To my wonderfully collaborative colleagues in the English Language Institute at Pikes Peak Community College, Colorado Springs, Colorado and to our colleagues in the adult ESL field who all so tirelessly and creatively pursue new ways to communicate the idiosyncrasies of the English language to all our students.

To ESL teachers and learners:

Over my years as an instructor in higher-education ESL programs and refugee ESL programs or as a private ESL tutor, I have developed handouts to help my students better comprehend the concepts and structures I was teaching. Most of my handouts were developed to supplement the texts I was using in academically-based ESL programs in which students enter with reading and writing skills. These handouts are not necessarily for beginning ESL students but rather for those intermediate and advanced students who are trying to refine the skills they already have and prepare themselves for higher education.

These handouts have proven to be very useful tools for my students; they have provided easy summaries of textbook information, often on one page, from which the students could more easily grasp an entire chapter. Having left my courses, many of my students have later told me that they have kept their handouts to aid them in more advanced, regular English classes.

This is not a comprehensive text but rather a selection of handouts developed in specific instances for particular concepts when the texts seemed to be lacking or my students were overwhelmed with information. I created these handouts to ease their frustration and facilitate their understanding. At the encouragement of a former colleague, I have assembled them in this book. Hopefully, you will find them useful in your own teaching or learning as well.

Since the first edition in 2014, I have created new handouts for the specific needs of new students. They are included in this second edition along with a new section of over 300 idiomatic expressions based on animals, the body, and work. Not only do these idiomatic expressions provide a glimpse into our culture, they add "color" to our communications with one another. The origins, meanings and sample sentences are provided in a user-friendly format and easy-to-understand language. I hope you find these new resources useful .

Patricia Nichols-Johnson, 2018

Tung Hai University, Taichung, Taiwan
Alaska Pacific University, Anchorage, Alaska
Master of Arts in Teaching: Bilingual and Multi-Cultural Education, APU
Refugee English School, San Antonio, Texas
Trinity Lutheran College, Seguin, Texas
English Language Institute/China
Pikes Peak Community College, Colorado Springs, Colorado
Tsinghua University, Beijing, China

TABLE OF CONTENTS

PART II: WRITING

PART III: READING

ABBREVIATIONS & ACRONYMS

PREFIXES, ROOTS, AND SUFFIXES

PART IV: PRONUNCIATION

INTRODUCTION TO ESSENTIAL ELEMENTS

PRONUNCIATION

INTONATION

STRESS & RHYTHM

PART V: IDIOMATIC EXPRESSIONS

TEXT CREDITS & COMMENTS

IMAGE CREDITS

PART I

GRAMMAR

These "framed" diversions randomly occupy otherwise blank pages and are
not listed in the Table of Contents.

A LIST OF COMMONLY USED ADVERBS

Adapted from http://www.core-corner.com/Web2/FreeDownload/k2qd717v_20090720.pdf

An ADVERB modifies (gives information about) a verb. This is a list of some of the adverbs that you can use to describe actions. An adverb gives information about *how, when,* or *where* the action takes/took place. There are many other adverbs that are not included on this list.

accidentally	crossly	gladly	nearly	reluctantly	sternly
afterwards	cruelly	gracefully	neatly	repeatedly	successfully
almost	daily	greedily	nervously	rightfully	suddenly
always	defiantly	happily	never	roughly	suspiciously
angrily	deliberately	hastily	noisily	rudely	swiftly
annually	doubtfully	honestly	not	sadly	tenderly
anxiously	easily	hourly	obediently	safely	tensely
awkwardly	elegantly	hungrily	obnoxiously	seldom	thoughtfully
badly	enormously	innocently	often	selfishly	tightly
blindly	enthusiastically	inquisitively	only	seriously	tomorrow
boastfully	equally	irritably	painfully	shakily	too
boldly	even	joyously	perfectly	sharply	truthfully
bravely	eventually	justly	politely	shrilly	unexpectedly
briefly	exactly	kindly	poorly	shyly	very
brightly	faithfully	lazily	powerfully	silently	victoriously
busily	far	less	promptly	sleepily	violently
calmly	fast	loosely	punctually	slowly	vivaciously
carefully	fatally	loudly	quickly	smoothly	warmly
carelessly	fiercely	madly	quietly	softly	weakly
cautiously	fondly	merrily	rapidly	solemnly	wearily
cheerfully	foolishly	monthly	rarely	sometimes	well
clearly	fortunately	more	really	soon	wildly
correctly	frantically	mortally	recklessly	speedily	yearly
courageously	gently	mysteriously	regularly	stealthily	yesterday

WHERE TO PLACE *ONLY*

Place *ONLY* immediately in front of the word that you want to restrict. If it is placed at the
end of the sentence, you are essentially restricting all the information in the sentence.
Pay attention as the meaning changes in the following example:

Only *I helped the hostess entertain her husband's guests last night.*

    Just me – no one else helped.

I **only** *helped the hostess entertain her husband's guests last night.*

    I didn't do anything else but help her.

I helped **only** *the hostess entertain her husband's guests last night.*

    I didn't help anyone else.

I helped the **only** *hostess entertain her husband's guests last night.*

    There was just one hostess.

I helped the hostess **only** *entertain her husband's guests last night.*

    I didn't help her with anything else but entertain the guests.

I helped the hostess entertain **only** *her husband's guests last night.*

    I helped her entertain only the guests her husband invited.

I helped the hostess entertain her **only** *husband's guests last night.*

    She just has one husband.

I helped the hostess entertain her husband's **only** *guests last night.*

    He didn't have very many guests.

I helped the hostess entertain her husband's guests **only** *last night.*

    I just did this for last night—no other night.

I helped the hostess entertain her husband's guests last night **only.**

    I just did this one thing for this one person at this one time.

HOW TO CHOOSE THE CORRECT ARTICLE

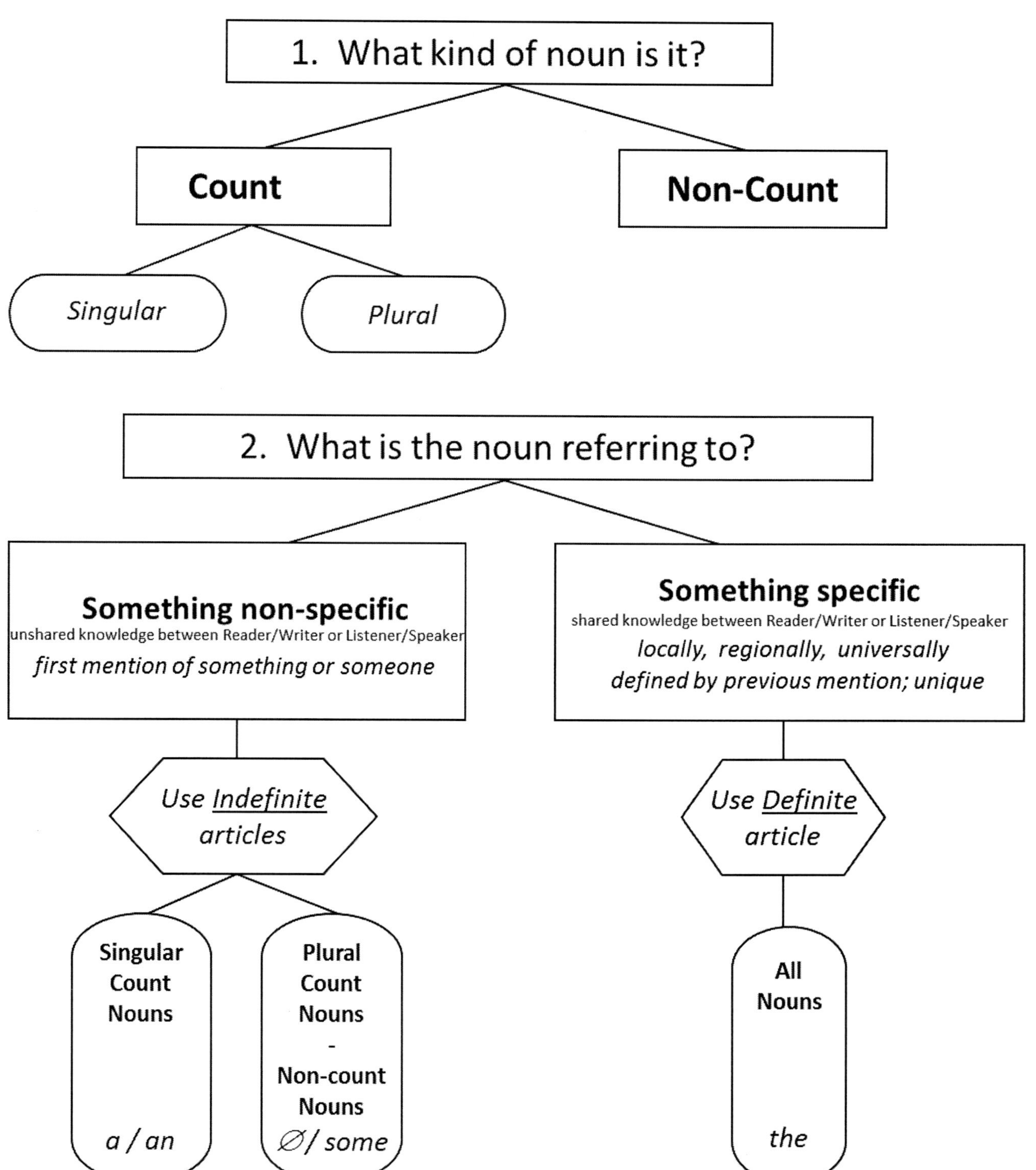

DEFINITE & INDEFINITE ARTICLES
[*a, an, the, some*, or *ø*]

	COUNT NOUNS		NON-COUNT NOUNS
	[SINGULAR] *a/an*	**[PLURAL]** *some/ø*	*some/ø*
INDEFINITE	There is a child in a park.		I saw some furniture in the window.
	An old man is on a bench.		Coffee and sugar are on sale today.
	Some birds are on some trees.		Some information isn't important.
	Some children are in parks.		Weather and some entertainment are usually part of TV news.
	Men don't understand women.		Air and water are necessary for survival.
	[SINGULAR] *the*	**[PLURAL]** *the*	*the*
DEFINITE	The child in the park is crying.		The furniture in her house is antique.
	The birds are blackbirds.		The coffee is not decaffeinated.
	The children are playing Frisbee.		I have the information she needs.
	The men and women on my team work together.		The weather is beautiful today.

CLAUSE COMPARISON CHART

ADJECTIVE CLAUSES	NOUN CLAUSES	ADVERB CLAUSES
◆ Function as **adjectives**	◆ Function as **nouns**	◆ Function as **adverbs**

1. They answer questions about nouns:
  • Which one?
  • What kind?
2. Use these introductory words:
  • Who
  • Which
  • That
  • Whose
  • When
  • Where
  • Whom
	1. They answer the question:
	  • What?
	2. Use these introductory words:
	  • That
	  • How
	  • What
	  • Why
	  • When
	  • Where
	  • If
	  • Whether
		1. They answer questions about verbs:
		  • When? (Time)
		  • Why? (Purpose/Reason)
		  • Shows contrast/opposition
		2. Use subordinating conjunctions as introductory words:
		  • Although
		  • Because
		  • If
		  • When
		  • And others . . .

They come after the noun they modify/describe: • She likes the *man* **that my sister dates.** • The *place* **where we got married** is special. • The *teacher* **who yells a lot** teaches that class. • She likes the *flowers* **that he brought.**	They go where a noun can go. They can be the: Subject of a sentence (**What she said** *isn't true.*) Subject complement (*My opinion* <u>is</u> **that you shouldn't go to the party.**) Object of a verb (*I* <u>wonder</u> **whether they're coming.**) Object of a preposition (*I'll think* <u>about</u> **how you can help us.**) Object of an adjective (*I'm* <u>sure</u> **that they talked to her.**) "If" clauses can only follow verbs or adjectives. They cannot be the subject of a sentence. (*I'm not* <u>sure</u> **if we have class today.**)	They can come before or after the main clause. *She stays late* **because she has a lot of work.** Use a comma between clauses when the adverb clause comes first. **Because she has a lot of work,** *she stays late.*

One of my students asked her husband to help her with an assignment using Adjective Clauses.

Her husband said, "The only clause I know is big and fat, wears a red suit, and lives at the North Pole."

ADJECTIVE CLAUSES: DELETING RELATIVE PRONOUNS

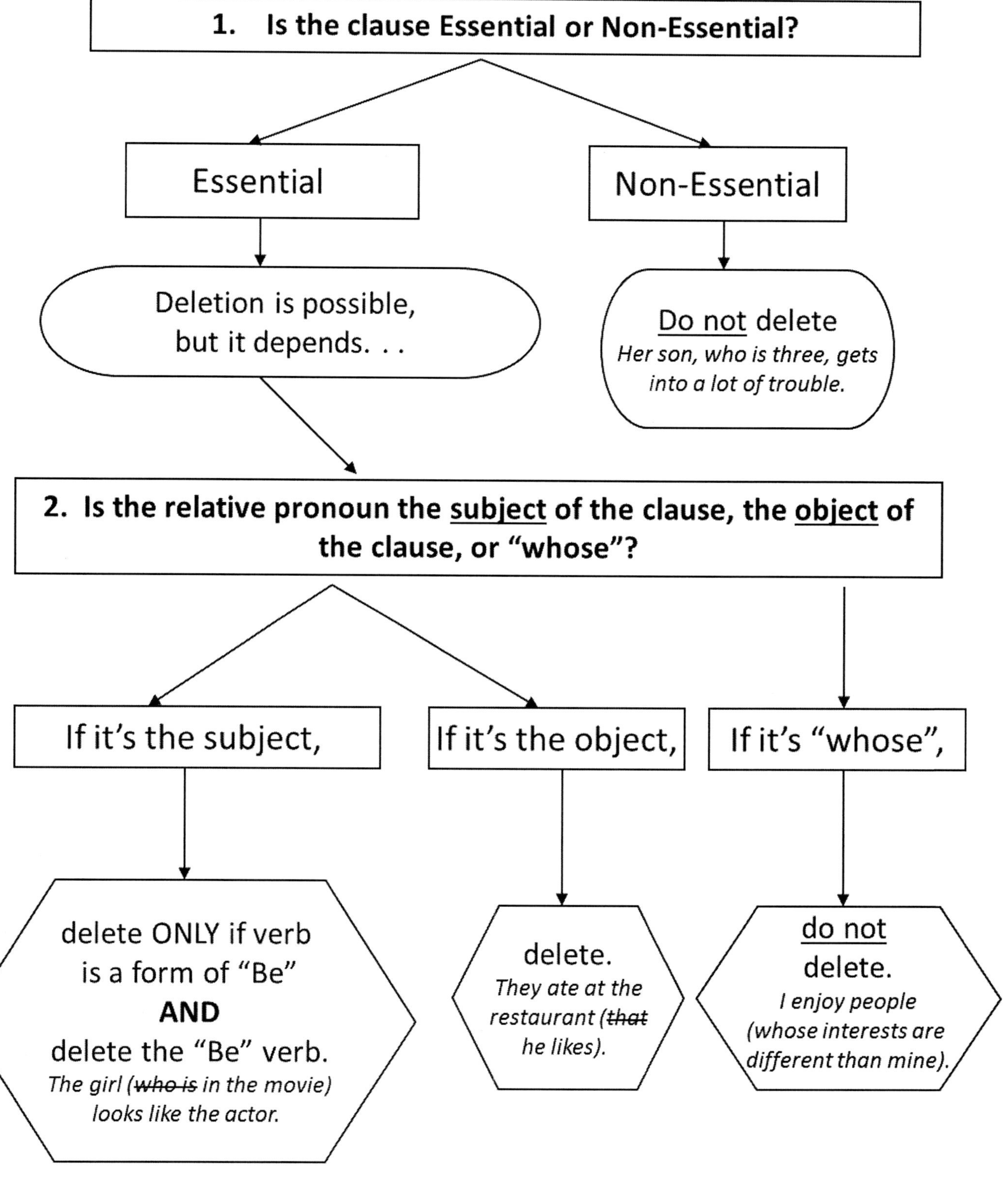

ADJECTIVE CLAUSES: THE COMMA RULE

	RESTRICTIVE CLAUSE (Essential) **No** Commas	**NON-RESTRICTIVE CLAUSE** (Non-Essential) Use Commas
HUMANS	__________that. . . __________who. . . __________whom. . . __________whose. . .	__________, who. . ., __________ __________, whom. . ., __________ __________, whose. . ., __________ (Proper Noun), who. . ., __________ (Proper Noun), whom. . ., __________ (Proper Noun), whose. . ., __________
NON-HUMANS	__________that. . .	__________, which. . ., __________ (Proper Noun), which. . ., __________

Use a comma before and/or after an adjective clause that modifies a Proper Noun. The Proper Noun is already identified, so the adjective clause is <u>automatically non-essential</u>. *Remember that Proper Nouns always start with capital letters even if they do not begin a sentence.*

*Joshua, **who graduates in June**, has received a job offer from Nike.*
*My daughter likes Joshua, **who graduates in June**.*

*Mrs. Carpenter, **whom I saw yesterday**, will retire this year.*
*I talked to Mrs. Carpenter, **whom I saw yesterday**.*

*Pedro Seguro, **whose daughter just moved to Portland**, is a great musician.*
*That great musician is Pedro Seguro, **whose daughter just moved to Portland**.*

VERBS AND ADJECTIVES THAT INTRODUCE NOUN CLAUSES

Adapted from Van Zante, Janis, <u>Grammar Links 3, A Theme-Based Course for Reference and Practice</u>, pp. 390-394, ©2005 Houghton Mifflin Co., Cengage Learning. Used with permission.

agree	find out about	care about	hear	admit	tell
believe	find out	feel	notice	announce	remind
decide		hope	see	answer	warn
doubt		wish	show	ask	yell
forget				comment	
guess	to be aware	to be afraid	to be obvious	complain	
imagine	to be certain	to be angry		declare	
know	to be clear	to be disappointed		demand	
realize	to be convinced	to be glad		explain	
remember	to be positive	to be happy		mention	
suppose	to be sure	to be pleased		promise	
think		to be sad		reply	
think about		to be sorry		say	
understand		to be surprised/at		scream	
wonder		to be worried/about			

NOUN CLAUSES: *THAT, WH-words, IF/WHETHER*

Adapted from Van Zante, Janis, Grammar Links 3, A Theme-Based Course for Reference and Practice, pp. 390-394, 397; ©2005 Houghton Mifflin Co., Cengage Learning. Used with permission.

I. Noun Clauses take the place of a noun; they always have a subject and a verb, and they can follow a select group of verbs and adjectives. Noun clauses answer the question, "What?" Noun clauses can begin with **that** or **why**, **where**, **when**, **what**, **who**, and **how** .

    A. **That** noun clauses can follow these verbs: *agree, doubt, guess, imagine, realize, show, understand, believe, feel, hear, know, remember, suppose, decide, forget, hope, notice, see, think*

    B. **That** noun clauses can follow these adjectives: *afraid, certain, glad, positive, sure, obvious, angry, convinced, happy, sad, surprised, aware, disappointed, pleased, sorry, worried*

    C. **Wh**-noun clauses can only follow these verbs: *decide, hear, notice, remember, understand, forget, know, realize, see, wonder*

    D. **Wh**-noun clauses can only follow these adjectives: *certain, clear, sure*

II. Noun Clauses can also begin with **if** or **whether.**   ALTHOUGH, **if** clauses can <u>only</u> be used in certain positions in the sentence, **whether** clauses can be used in <u>all</u> noun clause positions.

    A. <u>ONLY</u> a **whether** clause can begin a sentence:
        1. [**Whether** he has dementia] isn't obvious to the family.
        2. [**Whether** she is single or not] is none of my business.

    B. <u>ONLY</u> *a* **whether** clause can follow the verb "Be"
        1. The issue is [**whether** the weather will cooperate with us].
        2. The question is [**whether** the work will be done on time].

    C. <u>ONLY</u> a **whether** clause can be the object of a preposition:
        1. I often think <u>about</u> [**whether** I will learn enough English to get a good job].
        2. I need to find <u>out</u> [**whether** she has come home or not].

    D. <u>BOTH</u> **if** clauses and **whether** clauses can be the object of a verb (as with **wh**-noun clauses):
        1. I wonder [**if/whether** they will come].
        2. I don't know [**if/whether** it's going to rain].
        3. I don't remember [**if/whether** she turned in her assignment on time].

    E. <u>BOTH</u> **if** clauses and **whether** clauses can be the object of only a few adjectives:
        1. I'm not <u>sure</u> [**if/whether** I'll ever reach my career goals].
        2. She's not <u>certain</u> [**if/whether** she will have time for tutoring].
        3. It's not <u>clear</u> [**if/whether** I get five days off or three days off].

VERBS THAT ARE FOLLOWED BY GERUNDS & INFINITIVES

(. . .) = optional

VERBS FOLLOWED BY INFINITIVES *(to + base form of verb)*		
1 **Verb + Infinitive**	**2** **Verb + Noun Phrase + Infinitive** [1] do not use "to" after Noun Phrase	**3** **Verb (+ Noun Phrase) + Infinitive** [1] "to" is optional [2] "for" is optional w/Noun Phrase [3] "for" <u>must</u> be used w/Noun Phrase [4] "for" changes meaning
agree aim appear attempt care claim decide decline deserve hesitate learn neglect pledge pretend seem struggle tend	cause command convince force hire order persuade remind tell trust warn have[1] let[1] make[1]	choose dare get help[1] promise beg (for)[2] expect (for)[2] like (for)[2] need (for)[2] prefer (for)[2] want (for)[2] would like (for)[2] arrange (for)[3] be relaxing (for)[3] can afford (for)[3] can't afford (for)[3] couldn't afford (for)[3] can't wait (for)[3] couldn't wait (for)[3] consent (for)[3] demand (for)[3] hate (for)[3] hope (for)[3] intend (for)[3] love (for)[3] manage (for)[3] mean (for)[3] offer (for)[3] pay (for)[3] plan (for)[3] prepare (for)[3] refuse (for)[3] wait (for)[3] wish (for)[3] ask (for)[4]

VERBS FOLLOWED BY GERUNDS (Base form of verb + ing)		VERBS FOLLOWED BY GERUND <u>OR</u> INFINITIVE
4 **Verb + Gerund**	**5** **Verb** **(+ possessive Noun Phrase)** **+ Gerund**	**6** [1]difference in meaning if Infinitive or Gerund is used [2]followed by Gerund **OR** Noun Phrase + Infinitive [3]followed by Noun Phrase + Infinitive without "to" **OR** followed by Noun Phrase + Gerund
admit be worried about	acknowledge	begin
be (in) capable of can't help	anticipate	continue
be accustomed to dream about	appreciate	hate
be afraid of finish	avoid	hesitate
be angry at/about give up	can't help	learn
be ashamed of go**	consider	like
be busy have a good time	delay	love
be certain of/about have a problem	deny	prefer
be concerned about have fun	discuss	regret
be critical of have problems	dislike	start
be discouraged about have trouble	don't mind	
be enthusiastic about include	enjoy	forget[1]
be familiar with it's no use	excuse	remember[1]
be famous for keep on	finish	stop[1]
be fond of lie there	imagine	try[1]
be glad about look forward to	include	
be good at quit	listen to	advise[2]
be good for resist	mention	allow[2]
be happy about sit around/there	mind	encourage[2]
be interested in spend money	miss	forbid[2]
be known for spend time	postpone	invite[2]
be nervous about stand there	practice	permit[2]
be perfect for succeed at/in	put off	require[2]
be proud of suggest	recall	teach[2]
be responsible for talk/think about	recommend	urge[2]
be sad about waste money	resent	
be sorry about waste time	talk about	hear[3]
be successful in	think about	notice[3]
be tired of ***go + gerund***	tolerate	observe[3]
be tolerant of *used for activities that don't usually involve hitting a ball:*	understand	see[3]
be upset about bowling	worry about	watch[3]
be used to bicycling		
be useful for camping		
dancing		
fishing		
hiking		
hunting		
jogging		
running		
shopping		
swimming		

GERUND & INFINITIVE CHART: SAMPLE SENTENCES

*optional

Column 1 examples: Verb + Infinitive

1. I have <u>agreed to explain</u> the assignment to you again.

2. Many students <u>struggle to understand</u> the use of gerunds and infinitives.

3. ____

4. ____

Column 2 examples: Verb + **Noun Phrase** + Infinitive

1. I <u>persuaded **him** to buy</u> a new car.

2. Please <u>remind **us** to set</u> our clocks ahead.

3. ____

4. ____

Column 3 examples: Verb + **(Noun Phrase)*** + Infinitive

1. She <u>had chosen **me** to go</u> on the trip before the year ended. She <u>chose to go</u> on the trip before the year ended.

2. I <u>need (for) **you** to see</u> me this afternoon. I <u>need **you** to see</u> me this afternoon.

3. My parents <u>couldn't afford **for me** to go</u> to college. My parents <u>couldn't afford to go</u> to college.

4. ____

5. ____

Column 4 examples: Verb + Gerund

1. I am <u>certain about spending</u> that much money. I have no doubts.

2. Have you <u>finished eating</u> your dinner?

3. During the summer, my husband and I always <u>go camping</u>.

4. ____

5. ____

Column 5 examples: Verb + **(Possessive Noun Phrase)*** + Gerund

1. She <u>appreciates following</u> the new schedule. She <u>appreciates **your** following</u> the new schedule.

2. I <u>enjoyed singing</u> the Christmas songs. I <u>enjoyed **your** singing</u> the Christmas songs.

3. ____

4. ____

<u>Column 6 examples: Verbs + Gerund **OR** Infinitive</u>

1. She <u>began to tell</u> the story. She <u>began telling</u> the story.

2. He <u>started to talk</u> while the instructor was speaking. He <u>started talking</u> while the instructor was speaking.

3. Did you <u>forget to mail</u> the letter? Did you <u>forget mailing</u> the letter?

4. I <u>allowed my **children** to stay up </u>late. I <u>allowed staying up </u>late on the weekends.

5. My friend <u>taught dancing</u>. My friend <u>taught **elderly people** to dance.</u>

6. I <u>heard **him** come</u> into the house. I <u>heard **him** coming</u> into the house.

7. ____

8. ____

9. ____

10. ____

INFINITIVES WITH *TOO* AND *ENOUGH*

TOO

= excessive (too much)

TOO **+ adjective+ [infinitive]** = *My boss is <u>too busy to see</u> me*
TOO **+ adverb + [infinitive]** = *He's driving <u>too fast to be</u> safe.*

ENOUGH

= satisfactory, OK, adequate

ENOUGH **+ Noun + [infinitive]**
Carol doesn't have <u>enough time to visit</u> her mother.
Adjective + ***ENOUGH*** **+ [infinitive]**
She is <u>good enough to win</u> the competition.
Adverb + ***ENOUGH*** **+ [infinitive]**
He is driving <u>slowly enough to be</u> safe.

TOO

= excessive (too little)

TOO **+ adjective+ [infinitive]** = *My son is <u>too short to play</u> basketball.*
TOO **+ adverb + [infinitive]** = *He's speaking <u>too softly to understand.</u>*

MEANING OF *TOO* & *ENOUGH* WHEN GRAMMAR IS NEGATIVE OR AFFIRMATIVE

GRAMMAR		MEANING
A negative statement using TOO + infinitive = an affirmative statement using ENOUGH + infinitive.		
The concert **doesn't** cost TOO much money for me to go.	**MEANS**	The concert **is** cheap ENOUGH for me to go.
She **doesn't** have TOO much homework to do tonight.		She **has** ENOUGH free time to do something else
He **is not** driving TOO fast to be safe.		He **is driving** slowly ENOUGH to be safe
An affirmative statement using TOO + infinitive = a negative statement using ENOUGH + infinitive.		
The concert **costs** TOO much for me to go.	**MEANS**	I **don't have** ENOUGH money to go.
She **has** TOO much homework to do tonight.		She **doesn't have** ENOUGH time to do anything else.
My son **is** TOO short to play basketball.		My son **isn't** tall ENOUGH to play basketball.

<u>BUILDING A NOUN PHRASE</u>

1. FLOWER

2. brave FLOWER

3. brave, beautiful FLOWER*

4. brave, beautiful new FLOWER

5. brave, beautiful new purple FLOWER

6. brave, beautiful new purple FLOWER (in my yard)

7. brave, beautiful new purple FLOWER (in my yard) [that is popping up out of the ground]

*(comma separates adjectives within the same category)

I just saw a ***brave, beautiful new purple flower (in my yard) [that is popping up out of the ground]***.
The ***brave, beautiful new purple flower (in my yard) [that is popping up out of the ground]*** is a crocus.

1. NOUN

2. Adj of opinion/NOUN

3. Adj of opinion,/adj of opinion/NOUN

4. Adj of opinion,/adj of opinion/adj of age/NOUN

5. Adj of opinion,/adj of opinion/adj of age/adj of color/NOUN

6. Adj of opinion,/adj of opinion/adj of age/adj of color/NOUN (phrase)

7. Adj of opinion,/adj of opinion/adj of age/adj of color/NOUN (phrase) [clause]

ORDER OF ELEMENTS IN A NOUN PHRASE

The words or groups of words used as subjects are called noun phrases. Noun phrases may also function as objects of verbs and of prepositions. However, in any noun phrase, there is a "customary" order for the determiners, adjectives, and other modifiers. Although there is a usual "customary" order, other orders are all possible (see variations on back). Within any given category, there can also be variation.

1. *pre-determiners:* all, both

2. *determiners:* a/an, the, these, your, John's

3. *expression of quantity:* seven, many, several

4. *intensifiers*: really, very slightly

5. *adjectives of quality, evaluation, opinion:* happy, sleepy, angry, expensive, handsome, intelligent, interesting

6. *adjectives of size, shape, condition, and weight:* short, big, small, square, little, well-used, broken, 14-oz. 1-pound

7. *adjectives of age:* old, young, modern, antique, new contemporary

8. *adjectives of color:* red, orange, greenish-white, gray-haired, blue-eyed, multi-colored

9. *adjectives of nationality or origin:* Mexican, German, Thai, Vietnamese, American (use adjective form of country name)

10. *adjectives of material (what something is made of):* silk, titanium, gold, cotton, wool, glass, leather, metal

11. *noun or noun phrase being used as an adjective:* baby, toy, book, tennis, clothes, grocery

12. *main noun in the noun phrase*

13. *phrase modifier:* **modifies #12**

14. *clause modifier:* **modifies #12 and #13**

This chart represents only a "customary" order. It is NOT absolute.

1. Categories #5 and #6 are frequently reversed: _big heavy_ logs   or _little fluffy_ pillow
                                                    6 5   5 6

2. Categories #6 and #7 are frequently reversed: _new 4-door_ car or _fashionable contemporary_ hat
                                                    7 6   6   7

1	2	3	4	5	6	7	8	9	10	11	12	13	14
All	the		really	strong	tall	young		Cuban			men	at work	who were fired—
Both	the	two	very	excited	small		black	French			poodles	in the car	that were barking
---	Some			beautiful	little	antique	purple	(see 13)	jade		rings	in Hong Kong	———————
---	A	few	slightly	heavy		old			wooden	tennis	rackets	In the attic	———————
---	Arnold's				narrow	new	silver	Austrian	titanium	sun	glasses	————	looked flashy

1. All the really strong tall (tall , strong) young Cuban men at work who were fired got other jobs quickly.

2. I own both the two very excited small black French poodles in the car that were barking.

3. While I was traveling, I bought some beautiful little antique (antique little) purple jade rings in Hong Kong.

4. I found a few slightly heavy old wooden tennis rackets in the attic.

5. Arnold's narrow new (new narrow) silver Austrian titanium sun glasses looked flashy.

The Past, present, and Future
were talking together at a party.
The conversation was intense.

PARTICIPIAL ADJECTIVES

the *ACTION*	*PRESENT PARTICIPLE MODIFIERS* Describe the person or thing that *CAUSES* a feeling	*PAST PARTICIPLE MODIFIERS* Describe the person or thing that *EXPERIENCES* a feeling
aggravate	aggravating	aggravated
alarm	alarming	alarmed
amaze	amazing	amazed
amuse	amusing	amused
annoy	annoying	annoyed
appall	appalling	appalled
astonish	astonishing	astonished
astound	astounding	astounded
bewilder	bewildering	bewildered
bore	boring	bored
calm	calming	calmed
captivate	captivating	captivated
challenge	challenging	challenged
charm	charming	charmed
comfort	comforting	comforted
compel	compelling	compelled
confuse	confusing	confused
convince	convincing	convinced
depress	depressing	depressed
devastate	devastating	devastated
disappoint	disappointing	disappointed
disgust	disgusting	disgusted
distract	distracting	distracted
distress	distressing	distressed
disturb	disturbing	disturbed
embarrass	embarrassing	embarrassed
enchant	enchanting	enchanted
encourage	encouraging	encouraged
entertain	entertaining	entertained
excite	exciting	excited
frighten	frightening	frightened
humiliate	humiliating	humiliated
infuriate	infuriating	infuriated
inspire	inspiring	inspired
insult	insulting	insulted
interest	interesting	interested
intimidate	intimidating	intimidated
intrigue	intriguing	intrigued
mislead	misleading	misled
mystify	mystifying	mystified
overwhelm	overwhelming	overwhelmed

the **ACTION**	**PRESENT PARTICIPLE MODIFIERS** *Describe the person or thing that **CAUSES** a feeling*	**PAST PARTICIPLE MODIFIERS** *Describe the person or thing that **EXPERIENCES** a feeling*
please	pleasing	pleased
puzzle	puzzling	puzzled
refresh	refreshing	refreshed
relax	relaxing	relaxed
reward	rewarding	rewarded
satisfy	satisfying	satisfied
shock	shocking	shocked
sicken	sickening	sickened
startle	startling	startled
surprise	surprising	surprised
tempt	tempting	tempted
terrify	terrifying	terrified
threaten	threatening	threatened
tire	tiring	tired
welcome	welcoming	welcomed
worry	worrying	worried

WHOOPS! YOUR PARTICIPLE IS DANGING!

PARTICIPIAL ADJECTIVE (PHRASE) **, SUBJECT + VERB.**

PARTICIPIAL ADJECTIVE (PHRASE)

An introductory participial adjective OR participial adjective phrase must describe the subject in the clause that follows it.

If it does <u>not</u> describe the subject that follows it, we call it a DANGLING PARTICIPLE; it just "hangs" there, useless.

Flattened by the powerful kick , the soccer player scored a goal.

Who or what was flattened?

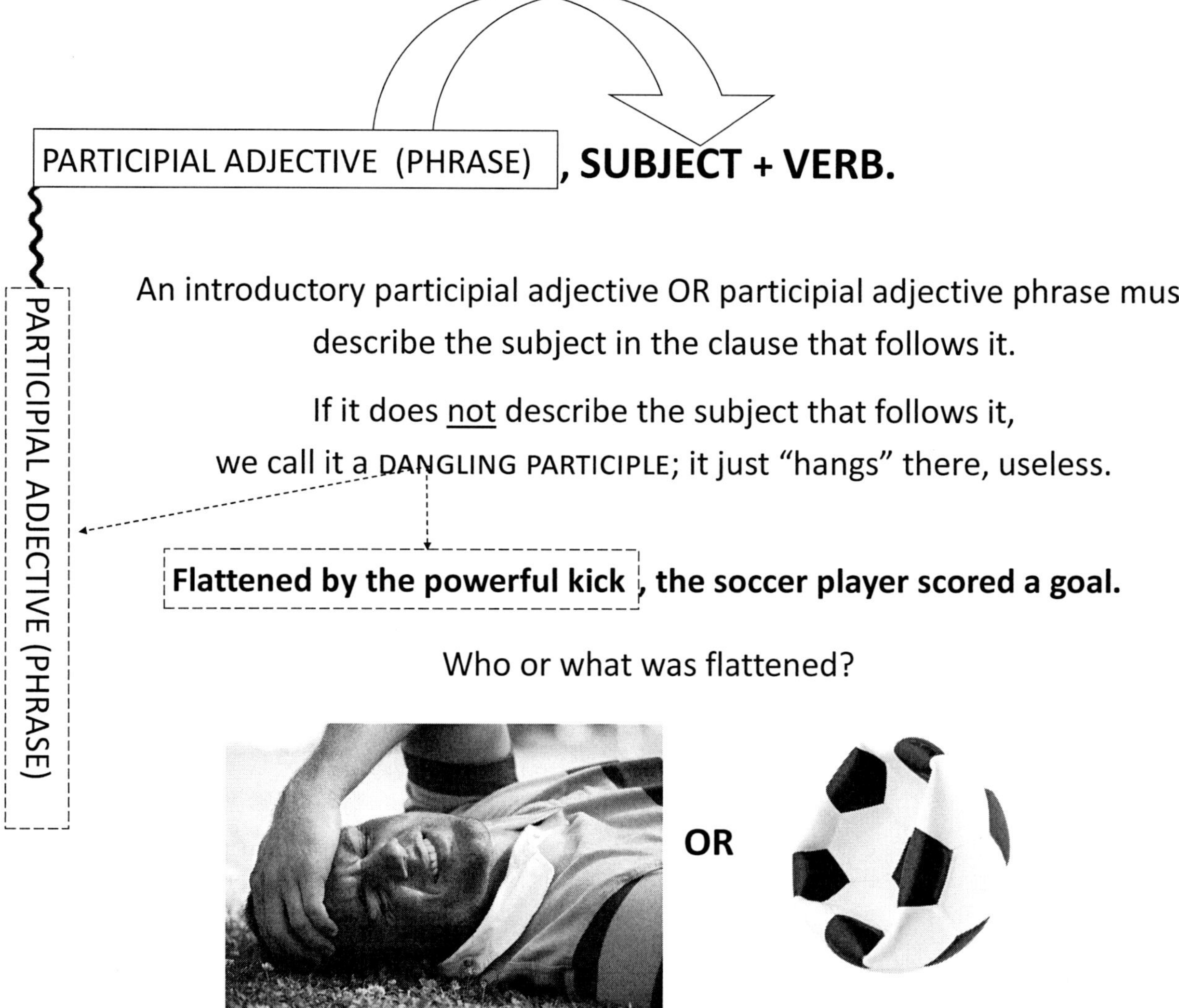

OR

✓**Flattened by the powerful kick, <u>the soccer ball</u> was replaced.**

Circle ✓ if correct or X if incorrect:

1. ✓ **X** Following the recipe carefully, my cake was a delicious success.

2. ✓ **X** Finally finished, my cake was a delicious success.

3. ✓ **X** Having gone to the store, the dinner was delicious.

4. ✓ **X** Having gone to the store early, my dad made a delicious breakfast.

5. ✓ **X** Written 20 years ago, the author finally decided to publish his book.

6. ✓ **X** Written 20 years ago, the book was finally published by the author.

7. ✓ **X** Frightened and confused, the immigrants were welcomed by the community.

8. ✓ **X** Sitting with a friend on a park bench, the moon appeared above the trees.

SAY THAT AGAIN!!!

1. Sleeping over is not the same as over sleeping.

2. Working hard is better than hardly working.

3. Quicksand can actually move quite slowly.

4. He can be upstanding even if he's not standing up.

5. Slow up and slow down mean the same thing.

6. Our noses run and our feet smell.

7. She's "awfully pretty" is a compliment; she's "pretty awful" is not.

8. To overlook means to ignore; to look over something means to review.

9. We call the third hand on a watch or clock the second hand.

10. Something can always be "out of whack" but never "in whack".

11. "Fat chance" and "slim chance" both mean "very little chance".

12. Doesn't "expecting the unexpected" make the "unexpected" expected?

13. Why don't we spell "phonetic" the way it sounds?

14. We put suits in a garment bag and garments in a suitcase.

15. Singers sing; clingers cling; ringers ring; fingers don't "fing".

16. Grocers don't "groce", and hammers don't "ham".

17. We seek advice from wise men but ignore wise guys.

18. Your house can burn up while it's burning down.

19. The plural of "tooth" is "teeth"; the plural of "booth" is not "beeth".

20. One goose, two geese; one moose, two moose. Really?

<u>CINQUAINS</u>

Machine
heavy metal
forge, grind, polish
noisy, busy, oily, dirty
Machine

Friend
loyal lady
forgiving, loving, laughing
friendly, delightful, content, calm
Friend

Boss
stern man
yell, tell, sell
angrily, carelessly, noisily
Boss

Supervisor
patient manager
listens, coaches, smiles, watches
kind, smart, easy, loyal
Supervisor

Follow this simple pattern to easily write creative
5-line poems using these parts of speech:
nouns, verbs, adjectives, and adverbs.

FORMULA FOR WRITING A CINQUAIN

Line 1 - One word title (**noun**) ——————————→ BOSS

Line 2 - Two words describing the title (**adjective + noun**) ——————→ STERN MAN

Line 3 - Three action words (**verbs with same form**) ——————→ YELL, TELL, SELL

Line 4 - Four words which describe the action words (**adverbs**) ————→ ANGRILY, CARELESSLY, LOUDLY, NOISILY,

Line 5 - Rename the title ————————————→ BOSS

Line 1 - One word title (**noun**) ——————————→ SUPERVISOR

Line 2 - Two words describing the title (**adjective + noun**) ——————→ PATIENT MANAGER

Line 3 - Three action words (**verbs with same form**) ——————→ LISTENS, COACHES, WATCHES

Line 4 - Four words which describe the title (**adjectives**) ————→ KIND, SMART, EASY, LOYAL

Line 5 - Rename the title ————————————→ SUPERVISOR

CINQUAINS - WORKSHEET

Sister lovely ____________ think, ____________, write ____________, smart, calm, ____________ Sister	Father ____________man play, ____________, work ____________, ____________, exciting, interesting Father
Life ____________lesson work, ____________, pay difficult, ____________, beautiful, ____________ Life	Girl beautiful ____________ smile, walk, love ____________, ____________, ____________, ____________ Girl
Happiness __________family find, keep, __________ cozy, __________, lively, __________ __________	____________ Beautiful body talking, __________, smiling wonderful, joyful, __________, __________ __________

CINQUAINS - STUDENT EXAMPLES

Student

smart learner

study, learn, think

intelligent, clever, good, cheerful

Student

Husband

sweet man

cook dinner, clean up, watch kids

busy, sleepy, helpful, kind

Husband

Kids

sweet children

study, help, hug

nice, good, lovely, mine

Kids

Seashell

happy home

swimming, playing, crawling

pretty, hard, long, wide

Seashell

Nephew

handsome boy

sleep, do, run

blonde, healthy, smart, tired

Nephew

Boyfriend

intelligent person

sing, study, eat

big, tall, strong, smart

Boyfriend

INDEFINITE PRONOUNS: *ONE, ANOTHER, SOME, OTHERS, THE OTHER/S*

There are **many animals** in the picture. (General)

1. Some are pigs.
2. Some are chickens
3. Others are sheep.
4. Some / others are horses.
5. Some / others are cows
6. Some / others are dogs.
7. Some / others are cats.
8. One is a bull.
9. Another / The other is a duck.

1. One is a duck
2. Another is a bull.
3. Some are chickens
4. Some / others are sheep.
5. Some / others are horses.
6. Some / others are cows
7. Some / others are dogs.
8. Some / others are cats.
9. Others / The others are pigs.

There are **23 animals** in the picture. (Specific)

1. Four are pigs.
2. Two are cows.
3. Two are cats.
4. Two are dogs.
5. Three are chickens.
6. Four are sheep.
7. Four are horses.
8. One is a bull.
9. The other is a duck

1. Four are pigs.
2. Two are cows.
3. Two are cats.
4. Two are dogs.
5. Three are chickens.
6. Four are sheep.
7. One is a bull.
8. Another is a duck.
9. The others are horses.

"Others" can **only** be used after "some" or a specific number has been mentioned.

"Another" can **only** be used after "one" has been mentioned.

"The other/s" can **only** refer to the remaining one/s mentioned in a group/list.

PREPOSITION TRIANGLE

(Although there are exceptions, *in, on*, and *at* generally follow this pattern.)

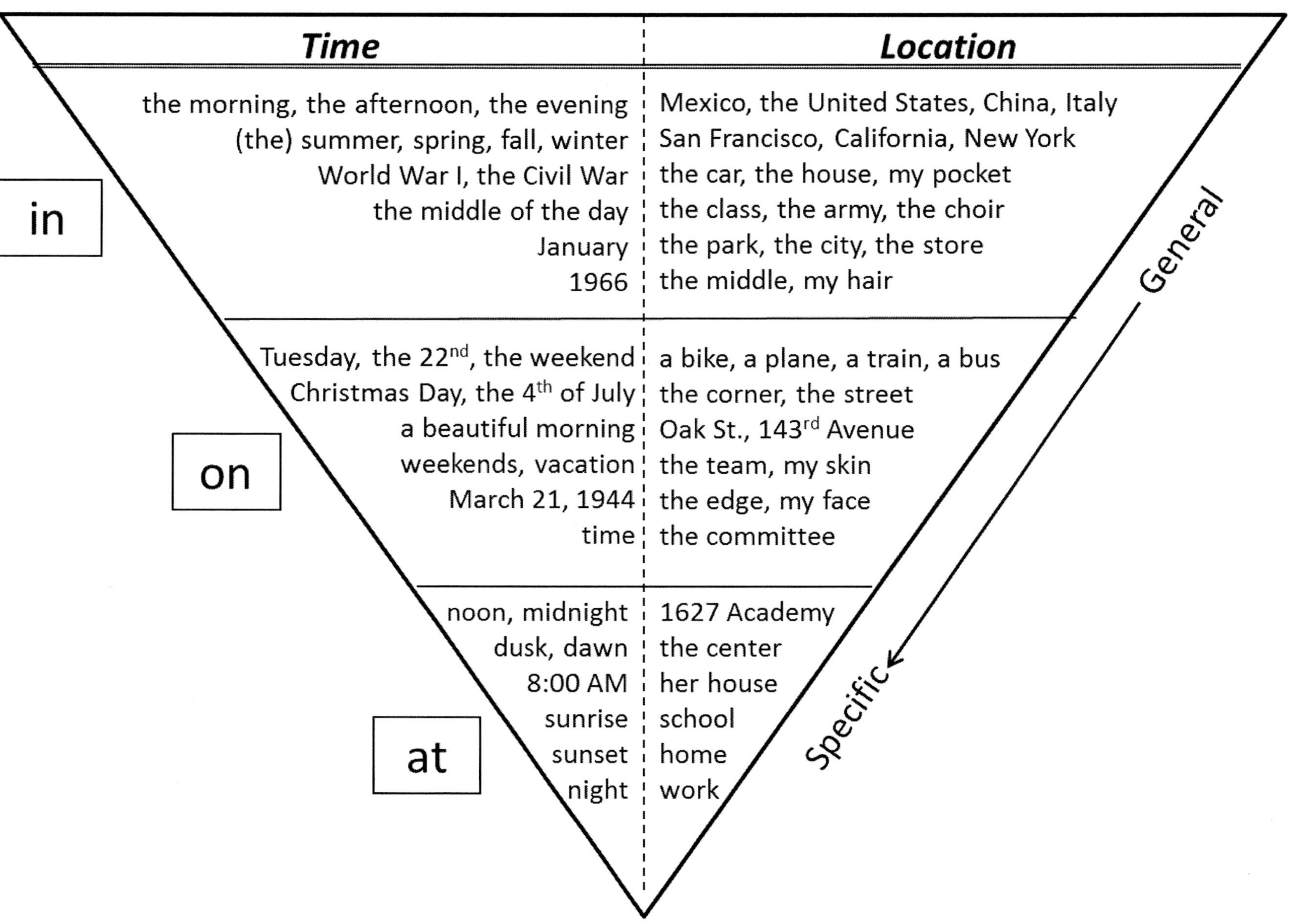

PREPOSITION TRIANGLE WORKSHEET

Use the "Preposition Triangle" to fill in the blanks in the following sentences with: *in, on, at.*

1. __________ the morning, I like to drink coffee.

2. My friend and I live _________ the same building.

3. I was born _________ February 19, 1963.

4. Please put the flowers _________ the middle of the table.

5. What time do we have to be _________ the bus?

6. We will travel _________ a car.

7. He has to be _________ work _________ 8:00 AM.

8. The managers get a holiday _________ Tuesday.

9. We will visit the coast _________ the summer.

10. My family and I will have dinner with my grandparents _________ Christmas Day.

11. Soldiers from many countries were fighting together _________ Afghanistan and Iraq.

12. We will meet _________ 1623 Jefferson Avenue.

13. Her store is _________ Fifth Avenue.

14. Write your name _________ the center of the circle.

15. The men are going to ride up the mountain _________ mountain bikes, but we will ride there _________ a car.

16. Please be _________ your appointment _________ Wednesday, the 14th _________ 7:30 AM because your surgery will be _________ the afternoon.

17. The pilot and the flight attendant were talking _________ the cockpit while the passengers got _________ the plane.

18. After the kids went hiking _________ the woods, they had scratches _________ their arms and leaves _________ their hair.

19. We visited China _________ 2008 for the Olympics.

20. She was born __________ San Francisco, California.

21. After work, those men play __________ an international soccer team.

22. __________ beautiful mornings, she likes riding __________ a horse __________ the beach.

23. We'll meet __________ the library __________ 11:30 AM __________ Friday.

24. He was born __________ April.

25. That building was constructed __________ 1856.

PREPOSITION TRIANGLE WORKSHEET— ANSWER KEY

1. ***IN*** the morning, I like to drink coffee.

2. My friend and I live ***IN*** the same building.

3. I was born ***ON*** February 19, 1963.

4. Please put the flowers ***IN*** the middle of the table.

5. What time do we have to be ***ON*** the bus?

6. We will travel ***IN*** a car.

7. He has to be ***AT*** work ***AT*** 8:00 AM.

8. The managers get a holiday ***ON*** Tuesday.

9. We will visit the coast ***IN*** the summer.

10. My family and I will have dinner with my grandparents ***ON*** Christmas Day.

11. Soldiers from many countries were fighting together ***IN*** Afghanistan and Iraq.

12. We will meet ***AT*** 1623 Jefferson Avenue.

13. Her store is ***ON*** Fifth Avenue.

14. Write your name ***AT*** the center of the circle.

15. The men are going to ride up the mountain ***ON*** mountain bikes, but we will ride there ***IN*** a car.

16. Please be ***AT*** your appointment ***ON*** Wednesday, the 14th ***AT*** 7:30 AM because your surgery will be ***IN*** the afternoon.

17. The pilot and the flight attendant were talking ***IN*** the cockpit while the passengers got ***ON*** the plane.

18. After the kids went hiking ***IN*** the woods, they had scratches ***ON*** their arms and leaves ***IN*** their hair.

19. We visited China ***IN*** 2008 for the Olympics.

20. She was born ***IN*** San Francisco, California.

21. After work, those men play ***ON*** an international soccer team.

22. **ON** beautiful mornings, she likes riding **ON** a horse **ON/AT** the beach.

23. We'll meet **IN/AT** the library **AT** 11:30 AM **ON** Friday.

24. He was born **IN** April.

25. That building was constructed **IN** 1856.

CLASSIFIERS

For counting "non-count" and some "count nouns"

a bag of...   **bags of...**

potato chips, cement, birdseed

a barrel of...   **barrels of...**

oil, sand, water, pickles

a basket of...   **baskets of...**

apples, flowers

a bottle of...   **bottles of...**

beer, wine, ketchup, tequila

a bowl of...   **bowls of...**

cereal, ice cream, chili, soup

a bunch of...   **bunches of...**

bananas, stuff, wire, clothes

a bundle of...   **bundles of...**

rope, newspapers, magazines

a can of...   **cans of...**

Coke, beer, orange juice, oil

a carton of...   **cartons of...**

milk, juice, cigarettes

a chunk of...   **chunks of...**

cheese, meat, wood

a crate of...   **crates of...**

oranges, engine parts, supplies

a cube of...   **cubes of...**

cheese, sugar, ice

a cup of...   **cups of...**

soup, coffee, tea, sugar

a dish of...   **dishes of...**

ice cream, spaghetti, stew

a flock of...   **flocks of...**

birds, geese, ducks, sheep

a gallon of...   **gallons of...**

milk, ice cream, gasoline, oil

a glass of...   **glasses of...**

water, juice, wine, beer

a head of...   **heads of...**

lettuce, garlic, cauliflower

a herd of...   **herds of...**

cattle, sheep

a jar of...   **jars of...**

mustard, screws, cotton

a loaf of...   **loaves of...**

bread

a mug of...   **mugs of...**

beer, coffee

an ounce of...   **ounces of...**

meat, oil

a pack of...   **packs of...**

cigarettes

a package of...   **packages of...**
cigarettes, filters, bandages, nuts

a pair of...   **pairs of...**
socks, shoes, pliers, glasses, jeans

a pallet (skid) of…   **pallets (skids) of…**
boxes, engines, newspapers

a piece of...   **pieces of...**
meat, bread, paper, plastic, pizza

a pint of...   **pints of...**
oil, milk, glue, soap, blood

a pitcher of...   **pitchers of...**
beer, milk, juice

a pot of...   **pots of...**
coffee, stew, soup

a pound of...   **pounds of...**
nails, coffee, meat, paper, fish

a quart of...   **quarts of...**
milk, oil, ice cream, juice

a roll of...   **rolls of...**
wire, toilet paper, gauze, bandages

a six-pack of...   **six-packs of...**
beer, Coke, juice

a slice of...   **slices of...**
bread, pizza, cheese, meat

a spool of...   **spools of...**
thread, wire, rope, cable

a stack of...   **stacks of...**
chairs, paper, clothes, towels

a stick of...   **sticks of...**
cinnamon, gum, dynamite

a tray of...   **trays of...**
food, surgical instruments

a tube of...   **tubes of...**
glue, toothpaste, caulk, grease

EXPRESSIONS OF QUANTITY

	Affirmative Statement *I have. . .*	Negative Statement *I don't have. . .*	Questions *Do you have. . .*
a, an (used with singular count nouns)	*a pen.*	*a pen.*	*a pen?*
Ø (used with non-count nouns or plural count nouns)	*paper.* *pens.*	*paper.* *pens.*	*paper?* *pens?*
some, any (used with non-count nouns or plural count nouns)	*some paper.* *some pens.*	*any paper.* *any pens.*	*any (some) paper?* *any (some) pens?*
a little (used with non-count nouns) **a few** (used with count nouns)	*a little paper.* *a few pens.*	(not usually used) (not usually used)	*a little paper?* *a few pens?*
a lot of (used with non-count nouns or plural count nouns)	*a lot of paper.* *a lot of pens.*	*a lot of paper.* *a lot of pens.*	*a lot of paper?* *a lot of pens?*
much (used with non-count nouns) **many** (for plural count nouns)	(not usually used) *many pens.*	*much paper.* *many pens.*	*much paper?* *many pens?*
enough (used with non-count nouns and plural count nouns)	*enough paper.* *enough pens.*	*enough paper.* *enough pens.*	*enough paper?* *enough pens?*
too much (used with non-count nouns) **too many** (used with plural count nouns)	*too much paper.* *too many pens.*	*too much paper.* *too many pens.*	*too much paper?* *too many pens?*

WHEN TO USE *SOME* AND *ANY*

Use *SOME* in affirmative statements

1. We want *some* more time to finish our work.

2. The manager wants *some* people to volunteer for the night shift.

3. *Some* nurses give the housekeepers a bad time.

4. I'd like *some* sugar in my coffee, please.

5. Yes, I'd like *some*.

6. I have cleaned *some* of the elevators on the floor, but not all of them.

7. Yes, I think we have *some* benefits with the new job.

8. ____

9. ____

10. ____

11. ____

12. ____

Use *ANY* in negative statements

1. We don't have *any* time to clean the walls.

2. She didn't get *any* new shoes.

3. Elias didn't get *any* donuts for the meeting.

4. Eva doesn't speak *any* Korean.

5. The new supervisor doesn't speak *any* Spanish.

6. ____

7. ____

8. ____

9. ____

10. ____

Use *SOME* in questions when you expect an affirmative answer.

1. Soraya, do you need *some* sugar?

2. Jung, do you have *some* change for the Coke machine?

3. We have *some* extra towels, don't we?

4. Do you have *some* people in your department who speak Spanish?

5. Does he have *some* trouble with the copy machine?

6. Would you like *some* more coffee?

7. ____

8. ____

9. ____

10. ____

11. ____

Use *ANY* in questions when the answer is uncertain

1. Are there *any* clean sheets in the room?

2. Did you have *any* fun at the party?

3. Is there *any* glass cleaner in the bottle?

4. Are there *any* paper towels in the dispenser?

5. Does the new supervisor have *any* patience with people?

6. Do we get *any* benefits with this job?

7. ____

8. ____

9. ____

10. ____

11. ____

QUANTITY - WORKSHEET

Instructions: In sentences 1-16, fill in the blanks with an expression of quantity to make a true statement about your native country. On lines 17-25, write your own true statement about your country using an expression of quantity.

1. There are _________________ foreigners in my country.

2. There's _________________ pollution in my country.

3. _________________ people own a car.

4. _________________ people have a television.

5. _________________ people have a telephone.

6. _________________ people have servants.

7. _________________ people use credit cards.

8. _________________ people are bilingual.

9. _________________ people have a college education.

10. People in my country eat _________________________ fish.

11. _________________ families have more than five children.

12. _________________ women work outside the home.

13. _________________ married couples have their own apartment.

14. There are _________________ divorces.

15. _________________ old people live with their married children.

16. There's _________________ opportunity to make money.

17. ____

18. ____

19. ____

20. ____

21. ____

22. ____

23. ____

24. ____

25. ____

WHEN TO ADD DO IN NEGATIVE STATEMENTS

1. When you want to make a statement negative, check to see if the main verb is a form of **BE** or uses the helping verb **HAVE** or a **modal**. If any of these are present, add "not" after **BE/HAVE** or the **modal**.

SUBJECT	PREDICATE			
	modal/BE/HAVE	**verb**	**object/subject complement**	**adverb phrase**
The lottery winner	*will*	buy	a new car	tomorrow.
The lottery winner	*will* **not**	buy	a new car	tomorrow.
The student	*had*	finished	all the homework	before class.
The student	*had* **not**	finished	all the homework	before class.
The women	*are*	carrying	baskets	on their heads.
The women	*are* **not**	carrying	baskets	on their heads.
His friend	*can*	climb	Pikes Peak.	
His friend	*can* **not**	climb	Pikes Peak.	
This grammar question	*is/was*		difficult to understand.	
The grammar question	*is/was* **not**		difficult to understand.	

2. **HOWEVER**, if there is <u>no</u> form of **BE,** the helping verb **HAVE,** or a **modal**, you will have to add The helping verb **DO** to make the statement negative. **DO** must show the tense of the original verb and agree with the subject. Add "not" <u>after</u> the correct form of **DO**. Return the main verb to its base form.

SUBJECT	PREDICATE			
	BE/HAVE/ modal	**verb**	**object**	**adverb phrase**
A tornado	----------	kills	many people in the village	every year.
A tornado		**does not** *kill*	many people in the village	every year.
The student	----------	completed	all the homework	before class.
The student		**did not** *complete*	all the homework	before class.
Antique planes	----------	make	a lot of noise	at the air show.
Antique planes		**do not** *make*	a lot of noise	at the air show.
My friend	---------	has*	three dogs.	
My friend		**does not** *have*	three dogs.	

Summary: Adding the helping verb *DO* in Negative Statements

- When you add **DO,** it will show the tense of the sentence and agree with the subject:
    *Present Tense = I, you, we they **do**; he, she, it **does***
    *Past Tense = I, you, we they, he, she, it **did***
    *Present/Past Progressive = is/are/was/were **doing***
    *Present/Past Perfect = has/have/had **done***

- Place "**not**" right after the correct form of **DO** and before the main verb.
    Do + not may be contracted to **"don't"**
    Does + not may be contracted to **"doesn't"**
    Did + not may be contracted to **"didn't"**

- In the sentence below, the main verb returns to its <u>base form, and we use the present tense of "DO"</u>:
  <u>**does**</u>

  *The tornado **kills** many people in the village every year.*
                    *==> The tornado **does** <u>not</u> **kill** many people in the village every year.*

- *When **HAVE** is <u>**not**</u> <u>a helping verb</u>, it follows the patterns with **DO**.

WHEN TO ADD **DO** IN *YES-NO* QUESTIONS

1. When you want to change a statement into a "yes-no" question, check to see if the main verb is a form of **BE** or uses the helping verb **HAVE** or a **modal**. If any of these are present, invert them with the subject.

SUBJECT	PREDICATE			
	modal/BE/HAVE	**verb**	**object/subject complement**	**adverb phrase**
The lottery winner	*will*	buy	a new car	tomorrow.
***Will** the lottery winner*		buy	a new car	tomorrow?
The student	*had*	finished	all the homework	before class.
***Had** the student*		finished	all the homework	before class?
The women	*are*	carrying	baskets	on their heads.
***Are** the women*		carrying	baskets	on their heads?
His friend	*can*	climb	Pikes Peak.	
***Can** his friend*		climb	Pikes Peak?	
The grammar question	*is/was*		difficult to understand.	
***Is/Was** the grammar question*			difficult to understand?	

2. **HOWEVER**, if there is <u>no</u> form of **BE**, the helping verb **HAVE**, or a **modal,** you will have to add the helping verb **DO** to change the statement into a "yes-no" question. **DO** must show the tense of the original verb and agree with the subject. Invert the subject with the correct form of **DO**. Return the main verb to its base form.

SUBJECT	PREDICATE			
	BE/HAVE/ modal	**verb**	**object**	**adverb phrase**
A tornado	----------	kills	many people in the village	every year.
Does a tornado *kill*			many people in the village	every year?
The student	----------	completed	all the homework	before class.
Did the student *complete*			all the homework	before class?
Antique planes	----------	make	a lot of noise	at the air show.
Do antique planes *make*			a lot of noise	at the air show?
His friend	----------	has*	three dogs.	
Does his friend *have*			three dogs?	

Summary: Adding the helping verb *DO* in *Yes-No* Questions

- When you add **DO,** it will show the tense of the sentence and agree with the subject:
    *Present Tense = I, you, we they **do**; he, she, it **does***
    *Past Tense = I, you, we they, he, she, it **did***
    *Present/Past Progressive = is/are/was/were **doing***
    *Present/Past Perfect = has/have/had **done***

- Place the correct form of **DO** in front of the subject.

- In the sentence below, the main verb returns to its <u>base form, and we use the past tense of "DO": **did**</u>

    *The student **completed** all the homework. ==> **Did** the student **complete** all the homework?*

- *When **HAVE** is <u>not</u> a helping verb, it follows the patterns with **DO**.

WHEN TO ADD **DO** IN *WH*-QUESTIONS

1. When you want to ask a *Wh*-question *about **the SUBJECT*** in a sentence, simply replace the subject with **who** or **what**. **Who/What** will always take the third person singular form of the verb.

SUBJECT	PREDICATE			
	modal/BE/HAVE	verb	object	adverb phrase
The lottery winner	will	buy	a new car	tomorrow.
Who	will	buy	a new car	tomorrow?
A tornado	----------	kills	many people in the village	every year.
What	----------	kills	many people in the village	every year?
The student	had	finished	all the homework	before class.
Who	had	finished	all the homework	before class?
The women	are	carrying	baskets	on their heads.
Who	is	carrying	baskets	on their heads?
The scary story	----------	frightened	the children.	
What	----------	frightened	the children?	
Antique planes	----------	make	a lot of noise	during an air show.
What	----------	makes	a lot of noise	during an air show?

2. When you want to ask a *Wh*-question about any ***information in the PREDICATE*** of a sentence, check to see if there is a form of **BE,** the helping verb **HAVE,** or a **modal.** If there is, invert the subject with the form of **BE/HAVE** or the **modal** and place a *Wh*-question word (***where, when, what***, etc.) at the beginning of the question.

SUBJECT	PREDICATE			
	modal/BE/HAVE	verb	object	adverb phrase
The lottery winner	will	buy	a new car	tomorrow.
What will the lottery winner buy tomorrow? **When will** the lottery winner buy a new car?		Answer: a new car Answer: tomorrow		
The student	had	finished	all the homework	before class.
When had the student finished all the homework? **What had** the student finished before class?		Answer: before class Answer: all the homework		
The women	are	carrying	baskets	on their heads.
Where are the women carrying baskets? **What are** the women carrying on their heads?		Answer: on their heads Answer: baskets		

3. **HOWEVER**, to ask a question about *the specific action in the PREDICATE*, invert the subject with the form of **BE**, the helping verb **HAVE,** or **modal** and replace the original verb with the helping verb **DO**, which must show the tense of the original verb. Add *what* at the beginning.

SUBJECT	PREDICATE			
	modal/BE/HAVE	**verb**	**object**	**adverb phrase**
The lottery winner	will	buy	a new car	tomorrow.
What will the lottery winner **do** tomorrow? Answer: buy a new car				
The student	had	finished	all the homework	before class.
What had the student **done** before class? Answer: finished all the homework				
The women	are	carrying	baskets	on their heads.
What are the women **doing**? Answer: carrying baskets on their heads.				

4. If the question is about *any other information in the PREDICATE*, you will have to add the helping verb **DO** if there is <u>no</u> form of **BE,** the helping verb **HAVE**, or a **modal**. **DO** must show the tense of the original verb and agree with the subject. Invert the subject with the correct form of **DO** and place a *Wh*-question word (*where, when, what*, etc.) at the beginning of the question.

SUBJECT	PREDICATE			
	modal/BE/HAVE	**verb**	**object**	**adverb phrase**
A tornado	----------	kills	many people in the village	every year.

Who does a tornado kill every year? Answer: many people in the village
What does a tornado **do** every year? Answer: kill many people in the village
When does a tornado kill many people in the village? Answer: every year
Where does a tornado kill many people every year? Answer: in the village

SUBJECT	PREDICATE			
	modal/BE/HAVE	**verb**	**object**	**adverb phrase**
The scary story	---------	frightened	the children	at the beginning.

What did the scary story **do?** Answer: frighten the children
Who did the scary story frighten? Answer: the children

SUBJECT	PREDICATE			
	modal/BE/HAVE	**verb**	**object**	**adverb phrase**
Antique planes	---------	make	a lot of noise	during an air show.

What do antique planes **do** during an air show? Answer: make a lot of noise
When do antique planes make a lot of noise? Answer: during an air show

Summary: Adding the helping verb *DO* in *Wh*-Questions

- When you add **DO,** it will show the tense of the sentence and agree with the subject:
  Present Tense = I, you, we they *do*; he, she, it *does*
  Past Tense = I, you, we they, he, she, it *did*
  Present/Past Progressive = is/are/was/were *doing*
  Present/Past Perfect = has/have/had *done*

- Place the correct form of **DO** in front of the subject; place the Wh-question word at the beginning of the sentence.

- In the sentence below, the main verb returns to its <u>base form, and we use the present tense of "DO"</u>: **<u>does</u>**

  *The tornado **kills** many people in the village every year.*

  ==> Where **does** the tornado **kill** many people every year?

- *When **HAVE** is <u>not</u> a helping verb, it follows the patterns with **DO**.

WORSHEET FOR ADDING **DO** IN NEGATIVE STATEMENTS, *YES-NO* QUESTIONS, OR *WH*-QUESTIONS

Instructions: Change each of the sentences below into:

1. a negative statement
2. a *Yes-No* question
3. a *Wh*-Question

Remember! Check to see if the verb tense and check for forms of **BE,** the helping verb **HAVE,** or a **modal** to decide whether or not to add the helping verb **DO.**

1. The student used Skype today.

____

____

____

2. She tries to use Skype everyday.

____

____

____

3. She usually wears a headset.

____

____

____

4. She had trouble with the internet connection.

____

____

____

5. She was very frustrated.

____

____

____

6. Other people tried to help her.

____

____

____

7. She was finally able to reconnect to the internet.

____
____
____

8. She might need to buy a new computer.

____
____
____

9. She <u>has to</u>* find a good bargain.

____
____
____

* "has to/have to" must follow the patterns with **DO**

10. She still likes to use Skype

____
____
____

Just think!

We could never do anything if we didn't have verbs.

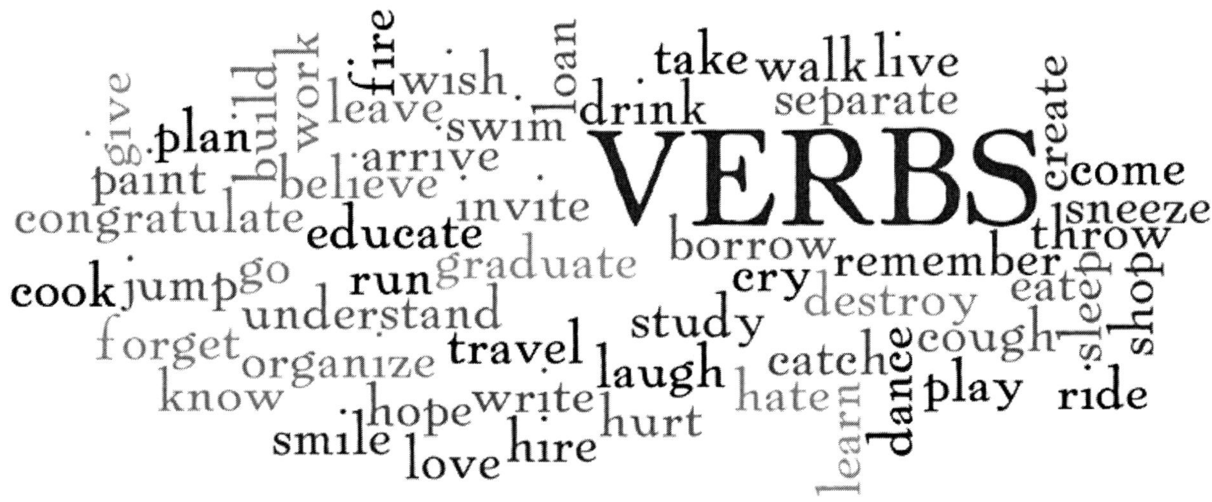

ACTIVE VOICE TENSE CHART

TENSE	=	TIME	+	ASPECT	FORM
SIMPLE PAST		Past		Simple	past form of verb
PAST PROGRESSIVE		Past		Progressive	was/were + verb + -ing
PAST PERFECT		Past		Perfect	had + past participle of verb
PAST PERFECT PROGRESSIVE		Past		Perfect Progressive	had + been + verb + -ing
SIMPLE PRESENT		Present		Simple	verb
PRESENT PROGRESSIVE		Present		Progressive	am/is/are + verb + -ing
PRESENT PERFECT		Present		Perfect	has/have + past participle of verb
PRESENT PERFECT PROGRESSIVE		Present		Perfect Progressive	has/have + been + verb + -ing
SIMPLE FUTURE		Future		Simple	will + verb
FUTURE PROGRESSIVE		Future		Progressive	will + be + verb + -ing
FUTURE PERFECT		Future		Perfect	will + have + past participle of verb
FUTURE PERFECT PROGRESSIVE		Future		Perfect Progressive	will + have + been + verb + -ing

PASSIVE VOICE TENSE CHART

TENSE	=	TIME	+	ASPECT	FORM
SIMPLE PAST		Past		Simple	was/were + past participle of verb
PAST PROGRESSIVE		Past		Progressive	was/were + being + past participle of verb
PAST PERFECT		Past		Perfect	had + been + past participle of verb
PAST PERFECT PROGRESIVE		Past		Perfect Progressive	had + been being + past participle of verb
SIMPLE PRESENT		Present		Simple	am/is/are + past participle of verb
PRESENT PROGRESSIVE		Present		Progressive	am/is/are + being + past participle of verb
PRESENT PERFECT		Present		Perfect	has/have + been + past participle of verb
PRESENT PERFECT PROGRESSIVE		Present		Perfect Progressive	has/have + been being + past participle of verb
SIMPLE FUTURE		Future		Simple	will + be + past participle of verb
FUTURE PROGRESSIVE		Future		Progressive	will + be being + past participle of verb
FUTURE PERFECT		Future		Perfect	will + have + been + past participle of verb
FUTURE PERFECT PROGRESSIVE		Future		Perfect Progressive	will + have + been being + past participle of

PASSIVE VOICE: REGULAR PASSIVES WITH "*BE*" AND "*GET*"

RECEIVER OF ACTION	+	**VERB*** *BE or GET* (*tense is indicated here*) *Although *BE* can be used for all passive voice, *GET* is used informally to show a major change in the lives of people.	+	**PAST PARTICIPLE** OF **MAIN VERB**	+	. . . *by* **_PERFORMER_** **OF ACTION** (optional)
1. The dog		was		washed		by the little boy.
2. The package		will be		delivered		by UPS.
3. The cookies		have been		baked		by school children.
4. The decayed tooth		had been		pulled		by the new dentist.
5. The flowers in my yard		are being		ripped out of the ground		by the dog.
6. Money		had been		happily received		by the Indonesian charity.
7. The bank robber		got		arrested		by the police.
8. My friend		is getting		married today		by the ship's captain.
9. The new employee		will get		fired tomorrow		by his supervisor.
10. My husband		had gotten		hired		by American Airlines.
11.						
12.						
13.						
14.						
15.						

PASSIVE VOICE: CAUSATIVE PASSIVE

PERSON *needing, requesting, or paying for a service*	+	VERB *GET or HAVE* (tense is indicated here)	+	OBJECT *receiving the service*	+	PAST PARTICPLE OF MAIN VERB	+	by PERSON/COMPANY *providing the service* (optional)
1. Mrs. Johnson		got		her hair		cut		by Pauline.
2. The children		will have		their teeth		cleaned		by our dentist.
3. My husband		is getting		our house		cleaned		by Eric.
4. Our neighbors		had		their house		remodeled		by House Renew.
5. Ivan		is going to have		his car		repaired		by the mechanic.
6.								
7.								
8.								
9.								
10.								
11.								
12.								
13.								
14.								
15.								

<u>USE THE PASSIVE VOICE WHEN. . .</u>

1. the performer of the action is unknown, unimportant, or unnecessary:

    a. *Jan's purse **was stolen** from the restaurant.*

    b. *The new library **was finished** about a year ago.*

    c. *I had an accident yesterday. The other car went through a red light and hit me. My car **was** completely **destroyed**.*

    d. *Reagan **was** first **elected** president of the United States in 1980.*

2. the receiver of the action is more important than the performer of the action:

    a. *Did you hear the news? Matt **was injured** slightly in the earthquake, but Jeff was OK.*

    b. *The package **was delivered** by Fed Ex at 4:00.*

3. you make general explanations/statements/announcements or write something scientific/technical.

    a. *Passengers **are asked** to refrain from smoking.*

    b. *Something **should be done** about the drug problem.*

    c. *Water **is formed** by the combination of hydrogen and oxygen.*

    d. *Lacerations and contusions on the victim's body **were received** in the accident.*

4. identification or responsibility is being avoided (by the performer of the action/writer/speaker) to protect the reputation or image of the performer of the action.

    a. *Mistakes **were made**.*

    b. *The cookies **have** all **been eaten**.*

5. the performer of the action is a general subject (*people, anyone, everyone*, etc.).

    a. *Long-standing social traditions **are observed** every holiday.*

    b. *Sometimes the reason for these traditions **can no longer be explained**.*

<u>Include the performer of the action in a "*by* phrase" when:</u>

- you want to provide extra information:

    *Many important scientific discoveries **have been made** by women.*

- you do not want to ignore important information about the performer of the action:

    *Radioactivity, for example, **was discovered** by Marie Curie in 1903.*

- you think the performer of the action is surprising or unexpected:

    *That picture **was painted** by a monkey.*

    *The poems in the book, <u>Heart Songs</u>, **were written** by a 12-year old boy named Mattie Stepanak.*

COMPARISON: ACTIVE VOICE, PASSIVE VOICE

ACTIVE VOICE

1. The sentence is about *the performer of the action*.

    a. The **weather** became violent.

    b. The **company** will hire more employees.

PASSIVE VOICE

1. Passive Voice sentences with *BE* or *GET* are about *the* receiver *of the action*--the direct object of the verb.

    a. **The computers** were broken by the students.

    b. **John** gets hired tomorrow.

    c. **Animals found during Hurricane Katrina** were all given new homes.

2. (Causative) Passive Voice sentences with *GET* or *HAVE* are about *the person needing, requesting, or paying for a service*.

    a. **Simone** got/had her nails done.

    b. **We** will have/get our air conditioner fixed.

    c. **Jason** has to get/have his jacket cleaned.

PASSIVE VOICE OR ACTIVE VOICE?

1. Simple Past	5. Simple Present	9. Simple Future
2. Past Progressive	6. Present Progressive	10. Future Progressive
3. Past Perfect	7. Present Perfect	11. Future Perfect
4. Past Perfect Progressive	8. Present Perfect Progressive	12. Future Perfect Progressive

Instructions: Put the number of the correct verb tense in the blank below; circle either AV or PV to indicate whether the verb in Active Voice or Passive Voice.

1.___________ av pv   The soldiers will be sent overseas.

2.___________ av pv   She drinks water everyday.

3.___________ av pv   Tom broke his leg.

4.___________ av pv   The fireman has been promoted to Captain of the department.

5. ___________av pv   They will have gone by September.

6. ___________av pv   Money is being given to the victims.

7. ___________av pv   We will be going to France next year.

8. ___________av pv   The children had been yelling loudly.

9. ___________av pv   Two million dollars was being donated to the Red Cross.

10. ___________av pv   The package will have been delivered by 4:00.

11. ___________av pv   The criminal will pay what he owes.

12. ___________av pv   Cats are chasing the dogs.

13. ___________av pv   The car was slowly lifted out of the water.

14. ___________av pv   The students had followed every instruction

15. ___________av pv   She was being quiet.

PUNCTUATION CAN CHANGE DINNER TIME

Let's eat! Children!

Let's eat, children.

Let's eat children.

FACTUAL/REAL AND HYPOTHETICAL/UNREAL CONDITIONAL STATEMENTS

Factual = **real,** actual, or true; general truths, habitual events, or <u>a real possibility</u> that these conditions and results did happen, do happen, or will happen

Hypothetical = **unreal,** not true; imaginary, impossible, contrary-to-fact, or unlikely conditions and results

Adapted from Van Zante, Janis, <u>Grammar Links 3, A Theme-Based Course for Reference and Practice</u>, pp. 346-379, ©2005 Houghton Mifflin Co., Cengage Learning. Used with permission.

	"IF" or CONDITION CLAUSE: Verb Forms	**RESULT CLAUSE: Verb Forms**
1. **Factual/Real Conditionals** ***Present* or *Future***	**Present or Future Conditions** *(Simple present, Present Progressive,* *Present Perfect, Present Perfect Progressive, can)* If I **have** time, If I **can** get off work, If anyone **calls**, (more uncertain) If anyone **should call**, If it **is** raining, Whenever I **have studied** hard enough,	**Present or Future Results** *(Simple Present, Simple Future, Be + going to* *Modals, Imperative)* I **clean** off my desk every night. I **will go to the movie with you**. please **take** a message. please **take** a message. we **should/could/would stay** home. then, I do fine on a test.
2. **Factual/Real Conditionals** Past	**Past Conditions** *(Simple Past, Past Progressive)* If the children **were crying** last night, If Alejandra was at the conference,	**Past Results** *(Simple Past)* they **had** a good reason. she probably **got** all the handouts.
3. Hope	Use grammar from "condition" clause: **Present** I hope (that) I have time I hope (that) I don't have to work. **Past** I hope (that) the children were not crying. I hope (that) Alejandra was at the conference.	<u>**Notes about Factual Conditional Statements:**</u> • **Then** can introduce the result clause but only if the result clause does not begin the sentence. *-If I have time after work, **then** I watch TV.* • **When** or **whenever** can replace **if** in the condition clause.

	"IF" or CONDITION CLAUSE: Verb Forms	RESULT CLAUSE: Verb Forms
4. **Hypothetical/Unreal Conditionals** *Present* or *Future*	**Present or Future Conditions** *(Simple Past, Past Progressive, could)* If I ***had*** time, If I ***didn't have to*** work, If Alejandra ***were*** at the conference, If my friends ***were*** in class, If I ***could*** see my friend, If it ***were snowing***,	**Present or Future Results** *(might/could/would + base form of verb)* I ***would*** clean off my desk every night. (*commitment*) I ***might*** go to the movie with you. (*possibility*) she ***would*** give me the handouts. (*commitment*) they ***could*** explain the homework to me. (*option*) she ***would*** explain the argument to me. (*commitment*) we ***could*** stay home all day. (*option*)
5. **Hypothetical/Unreal Conditionals** *Past*	**Past Conditions** *(Past Perfect, Past Perfect Progressive,* *could have + pp)* If Alejandra ***had been*** at the conference,	**Past Results** *(might/could/would + have + past participle)* she ***might/could/would*** have given me the handouts.
6. <u>**Wish**</u>	**Use grammar from "condition" clause:** **Present/Future** I wish (that) I had time to go tomorrow. I wish (that) I didn't have to work. I wish (that) Jennifer were in class today. I wish (that) my friends were in class today. **Past** I wish (that) Alejandra had been at the conference**.**	<u>**Notes about Hypothetical Conditional Statements:**</u> • ***Then*** can introduce the result clause but only if the result clause does not begin the sentence. *-If I had time after work, **then** I would watch TV.* • You <u>cannot</u> use ***when*** or ***whenever*** to replace ***if*** in the condition clause of a hypothetical statement.

EXPRESSING FUTURE EVENTS

Adapted from Van Zante, Janis, Grammar Links 3, A Theme-Based Course for Reference and Practice, pp. 82-115, ©2005 Houghton Mifflin Co., Cengage Learning. Used with permission.

Looking Ahead to the Future				Looking Back from the Future	

Promises Offers Requests Refusals	Intentions Plans	Predictions Expectations	Scheduled Events	Events completed by a future time or in a future time period	Events continuing up to a future time or for a future time period
	be + going to + V	(distant) Will + V	Simple Present	Future Perfect • will + have + Vpp • going to + have + Vpp	Future Perfect Progressive • will have + **been** + V-ing • be + going to + have + **been** + V-ing
will + V	(immediate) be + about to + V	(immediate) • be + going to + V • be + about to + V	Present Progressive		
	Present Progressive		be + going to + V		
	Over a **period** of time • will + V • will + **be** + V-ing • be + going to + V • be + going to + **be** + V-ing At a **moment** of time • Beginning: will, be going to + V • Continuing through: will + **be** + V-ing		(formal) will + V	**Sample Sentences** 1. 2. 3. 4. 5. 6. 7.	

"If I knew a secret, I could write it in my diary and lock it."

IRREGULAR VERBS

BASE FORM	SIMPLE PAST	PAST PARTICIPLE	BASE FORM	SIMPLE PAST	PAST PARTICIPLE
be	was/were	been	**fight**	fought	fought
beat	beat	beaten	**find**	found	found
become	became	become	**fit**	fit	fit
begin	began	begun	**flee**	fled	fled
bend	bent	bent	**fly**	flew	flown
bet	bet	bet	**forbid**	forbade	forbidden
bind	bound	bound	**forecast**	forecast/-ed	forecast/-ed
bite	bit	bitten	**forget**	forgot	forgotten
bleed	bled	bled	**forgive**	forgave	forgiven
blow	blew	blown	**freeze**	froze	frozen
break	broke	broken	**get**	got	gotten
bring	brought	brought	**give**	gave	given
broadcast	broadcast	broadcast	**go**	went	gone
build	built	built	**grind**	ground	ground
burn	burned/burnt	burned/burnt	**grow**	grew	grown
burst	burst	burst	**hang**	hung	hung
buy	bought	bought	**have**	had	had
catch	caught	caught	**hear**	heard	heard
choose	chose	chosen	**hide**	hid	hidden
come	came	come	**hit**	hit	hit
cost	cost	cost	**hold**	held	held
creep	crept	crept	**hurt**	hurt	hurt
cut	cut	cut	**keep**	kept	kept
deal	dealt	dealt	**know**	knew	known
dig	dug	dug	lay	laid	laid
dive	dove/dived	dived	lead	led	led
do	did	done	leap	leapt/-ed	leapt/-ed
draw	drew	drawn	learn	learnt/-ed	learnt/-ed
dream	dreamt/-ed	dreamt/-ed	leave	left	left
drink	drank	drunk	lend	lent	lent
drive	drove	driven	let	let	let
eat	ate	eaten	lie	lay	lain
fall	fell	fallen	light	lit	lit
feed	fed	fed	lose	lost	lost
feel	felt	felt	make	made	made

BASE FORM	SIMPLE PAST	PAST PARTICIPLE	BASE FORM	SIMPLE PAST	PAST PARTICIPLE
mean	meant	meant	**stand**	stood	stood
meet	met	met	**steal**	stole	stolen
mistake	mistook	mistaken	**stick**	stuck	stuck
pay	paid	paid	**sting**	stung	stung
prove	proved	proven/-ed	**stink**	stank	stunk
put	put	put	**strike**	struck	struck
quit	quit	quit	**swear**	swore	sworn
read	read	read	**sweep**	swept	swept
rid	rid	rid	**swell**	swelled	swollen/-ed
ride	rode	ridden	**swim**	swam	swum
ring	rang	rung	**swing**	swung	swung
rise	Rose	risen	**take**	took	taken
run	ran	run	**teach**	taught	taught
say	said	said	**tear**	tore	torn
see	saw	seen	**tell**	told	told
seek	sought	sought	**think**	thought	thought
sell	sold	sold	**throw**	threw	thrown
send	sent	sent	**understand**	understood	understood
set	set	set	**upset**	upset	upset
sew	sewed	sewn/sewed	**wake**	woke	woken
shake	shook	shaken	**wear**	wore	worn
shave	shaved	shaven	**weave**	woven	woven
shine	shone	shone	**weep**	wept	wept
shoot	shot	shot	**wet**	wet	wet
show	showed	shown	**win**	won	won
shrink	shrank	shrunk	**wind**	wound	wound
shut	shut	shut	**withdraw**	withdrew	withdraw
sing	sang	sung	**write**	wrote	written
sink	sank	sunk			
sit	sat	sat			
sleep	slept	slept			
speak	spoke	spoken			
speed	sped	sped			
spend	spent	spent			
spin	spun	spun			
split	split	split			
spread	spread	spread			
spring	sprang	sprung			

PERFECT MODALS

Adapted from Van Zante, Janis, Grammar Links 3, A Theme-Based Course for Reference and Practice, pp. 293-300, ©2005 Houghton Mifflin Co., Cengage Learning. Used with permission.

MODALS OF CERTAINTY

(used to express your certainty about what did or did not happen in the past)

Very Certain

must have + pp*	must **not** have + pp
has/have to have + pp	could **not** have + pp
has/have got to have + pp	can**not** have + pp

Certain

should have + pp	should **not** have + pp
ought to have + pp	

NOT very certain

may have + pp	may **not** have + pp
might have + pp	might **not** have + pp

*Past Participle

MODALS OF COMMENTARY

(used to express your opinion about what did or did not happen in the past)

Suggestion

could have + pp

Advice/Opinion *(weak)*

should have + pp	should **not** have + pp
ought to have + pp	

Expectation

was/were supposed to . . .	was/were **not** supposed to . . .
was/were to . . .	was/were **not** to . . .

Warning *(strong)*

had better have + pp	had better **not** have + pp

Prohibition

could **not** . . .

was/were **not** allowed to . . .

Necessity	**Lack of Necessity**
had to . . .	did **not** have to . . .

"Shoulda, coulda, woulda!"

This is often the frustrated response of someone
who is tired of someone else telling him, "You
should have done. . .," "You could have done . . .,"
or "I would have done. . . if I were you."

2-WORD PHRASAL VERB CHART

This list shows **only some** of the most common phrasal verbs.
More complete lists are available on the internet or in books specifically dedicated to Phrasal Verbs.

A phrasal verb is a **verb + a preposition or adverb** which creates a meaning different from the original verb. (**run into** = meet)

1. Some phrasal verbs do not take a direct object ⟶ He suddenly **showed up**.
2. Some phrasal verbs can take a <u>direct object</u> ⟶ He **made up** the story.
   a. Some of these combinations can be separated:
      - He **made** <u>the story</u> **up**. He **made up** <u>the story</u>.
      - I **looked up** <u>the phone number</u>. I **looked** <u>the phone number</u> **up**.
      - However, you must put the object between the verb and the preposition **if** the object is a pronoun:
        She **looked** <u>it</u> **up**. ~~She **looked up** it.~~
   b. Some of these combinations **can only be** separated:
      - I **talked** <u>my teacher</u> **into** letting me do my homework later.
   c. Some of these combinations **cannot be** separated:
      - I **ran into** <u>my son's soccer coach</u> last night at a party. ~~I **ran** my son's soccer coach **into** last night at a party.~~
      - She **looked into** <u>the situation</u>. ~~She **looked** the situation **into**.~~

X*= a phrasal verb which takes an object and can **only be separable** (verb + object + preposition/adverb)

VERB	OBJECT?	SEPARABLE?	at	about	away	back	behind	by	down	for	from	in	into	off	on	out	over	through	to	up
Act																X				X
Ask	yes	yes														X	X*			
Back					X				X					X		X				X
Back	yes												X				X			X
Back	yes	yes											X*							X
Blow																	X			X
Blow	yes	yes												X						X
Break									X			X				X				X

VERB	OBJECT?	SEPARABLE?	at	about	away	back	behind	by	down	for	from	in	into	off	on	out	over	through	to	up
Break	yes												X					X		
Break	yes	yes							X						X		X			X
Bring	yes	yes				X							X			X	X	X		X
Burn	yes	yes			X				X							X				X
Call	yes										for						X				
Call	yes	yes				X									X		X			X
Care	yes									X										
Carry																X				
Carry	yes															X				
Carry	yes	yes														X	X			
Check	yes									X			X							
Check	yes	yes								X*					X	X				
Cheer	yes	yes																		X
Clear	yes	yes			X											X				X
Close	yes	yes							X							X				X
Come					X	X			X			X		X	X	X	X		X	X
Count	yes														X					
Cross	yes	yes													X	X				
Cut												X								X
Cut	yes	yes			X	X			X					X		X		X*		X
Dig	yes												X							X
Dig	yes	yes																		X
Do	yes	yes															X			X
Dress									X											X
Drop						X		X					X			X	X			
Drop	yes							X												
Drop	yes	yes												X						

VERB	OBJECT?	SEPARABLE?	at	about	away	back	behind	by	down	for	from	in	into	off	on	out	over	through	to	up
Eat												X				X				
Eat	yes	yes																		X
End	yes											X								
Fall						X	X		X			X				X				
Fall	yes						X			X	X		X	X			X	X		
Figure	yes	yes														X				
Fill	yes	yes										X				X				X
Find	yes	yes														X				
Fix	yes	yes																		X
Get					X	X		X	X											X
Get	yes		X				X					X	X	X	X		X	X		
Get	yes	yes				X														
Give												X				X				X
Give	yes	yes			X	X										X				X
Go					X				X			X		X		X				
Go	yes						X	X		X							X	X		
Hand	yes	yes				X			X			X				X	X			
Hang						X	X					X			X	X				
Hang	yes	yes														X				X
Hold															X	X				X
Hold	yes	yes				X			X											X
Iron																X				
Keep					X	X	X													X
Keep	yes								X		X				X					
Keep	yes	yes			X							X				X				
Kick						X						X								
Lay	yes				X				X					X						
Lay	Yes	Yes												X						

VERB	OBJECT?	SEPARABLE?	at	about	away	back	behind	by	down	for	from	in	into	off	on	out	over	through	to	up
Let																				X
Let	yes	yes							X							X				
Look					X	X										X				
Look	yes		X				X				X		X							
Look	yes	yes															X	X		X
Make	yes																X	X		X
Make																				X
Mix	yes	yes										X								X
Open																				X
Pass					X											X				
Pass	yes														X					
Pass	yes	yes				X										X	X			X
Pay	yes									X			X			X				
Pay	yes	yes				X			X						X	X				X
Pick	yes															X	X	X		
Pick	yes	yes														X				X
Point	yes	yes														X				
Pop												X					X			X
Pop	yes							X					X							
Pop	yes	yes														X				
Pull					X	X											X	X		
Pull	yes													X	X			X		
Pull	yes	yes												X	X	X				
Put	yes														X					
Put	yes	yes			X	X			X			X				X	X		X	X
Quiet									X											
Run					X											X	X			

VERB	OBJECT?	SEPARABLE?	at	about	away	back	behind	by	down	for	from	in	into	off	on	out	over	through	to	up
Run	yes							X	X	X			X	X				X		X
Run	yes	yes						X*												
Sign													X	X		X				X
Sign	yes												X							
Sign	yes	yes			X												X			
Sleep													X				X			
Slow	yes	yes							X											X
Stand																	X			
Stand	yes						X	X			X				X					
Stay					X	X										X	X			X
Stay	yes						X					X		X	X			X		
Take	yes	yes			X	X			X		X		X	X	X	X			X
Talk	yes			X															X	
Talk	yes	yes											X*			X	X			X
Think	yes			X																
Think	yes	yes														X	X			X
Throw																				X
Throw	yes	yes			X	X			X							X	X			
Turn	yes	yes				X			X					X	X	X				X
Wait	yes									X						X	X			
Wake	yes	yes																		X
Wear																X	X			
Wear	yes	yes														X				
Work																X				
Work	yes	yes														X		X		
Write	yes			X																
Write	yes	yes				X*				X		X				X				X

PHRASAL VERBS - WORKSHEET #1

Use the Phrasal Verb Chart to help you fill in the following blanks with the appropriate preposition or adverb. If you're not sure, check the meaning in a dictionary or www.dictionary.com

1. (ask) If you're interested in that girl, you should ask her _________ or ask her_________. That way, you would get to know her better.

2. (back) The truck should not back _________ anymore; otherwise, it will back_________ the store window.

3. (blow) My friend blew _________ yesterday, so I'll stay away from her until the whole issue blows _________.

4. (call) That young man wants to call _________ Susan at 8:00 tomorrow night. He called her _________ and asked her if that would be all right.

5. (check) Please check _________ the new list of items in the store room, and check _________ the ones we need in the office.

6. (clear/close) The security guard will clear _________ the people and close _________ the store.

7. (come) The handsome, rich man in the book said, "Come _________ with me to the Bahamas, and we'll get married when we come _________."

8. (count/cross) You can count _________ me to cross _________ all the people who will not be coming to the party.

9. (fall) The sergeant told his soldiers to fall _________ line because he didn't want them to fall _________ or fall _________ any of the big rocks on the side of the road.

10. (get) Let's get _________ for a few days, and we can do all these house projects when we get _________.

11. (figure/find) If you haven't already figured _________ the answer to the question, I can help you find it _________.

12. (give) Don't give _________ to their demands! We must not give _________ any of our intentions, and we certainly cannot give _________.

13. (keep) The mom encouraged her small son to keep _________, and she asked the other noisy kids to keep _________ .

14. (make) She can't make _________ what the fine print says in that document, so they will probably have to make _________ the information.

15. (mix) When you're making this recipe, mix _________ all the ingredients first, and then mix it all _________.

16. (pass) Her father passed _________, and then he passed _________.

17. (pick) Pick _________ all those clothes in the box and then pick _________ the ones you want to take with you.

18. (put) Put the dog_________ , and then put him _________for the night.

19. (run) I just ran _________ my friend at the bank. Because he's running _________ the office of Mayor, he has run _________ his credit card bill and is now arguing with the bank teller about the charges.

20. (stand) In her political campaign, she has decided to stand _________ the new health care changes, so she needs her ideas to stand _________ in her campaign ads.

21. (stay) Because my childhood friend had driven a long way to visit me, I asked her to stay _________ and told her we could stay _________ late and share our old memories.

22. (talk) That unhappy teenager always talks _________ her friends but doesn't talk _________ them in order to explain why she's upset.

23. (think) The children thought _________ that story after they thought _________ the trouble they were in.

24. (work) I like to work _________ problems while I work _________ at the gym.

SYNONYMS FOR PHRASAL VERBS - WORKSHEET #1

1. ask out = ask someone on a date or to a social event
   ask over = ask someone to come where you live

2. back up = move/drive/walk backwards, reverse
   back into = move/drive/walk backwards enough to hit a structure or person

3. blow up = get angry quickly
   blow over = disappear (a problem/issue), become resolved, lessen

4. call on = visit
   call up = use the telephone to call someone

5. check out = review
   check off = put a check mark next to an item on a list

6. clear out = remove everyone/everything; ask everyone to leave a space
   close up = close a space to the public

7. come away = ask another person to leave quickly to a distant place
   come back = return

8. count on = rely, trust
   cross out/off = eliminate, put a line through

9. fall into/in = get in line behind one another
   fall on/over = stumble over, trip

10. get away = go on a holiday/vacation
    get back = return

11. figure out = solve, determine, solve internally within someone's own head
    find out = discover, solve externally through research and inquiry

12. give in = relent, agree finally
    give away = disclose, reveal, share
    give up = cease, surrender, quit

13. keep up = stay close
    keep away = stay at a distance

14. make out = see, discover, identify, recognize
make up = create something not necessarily true, conjure, fabricate a story

15. mix in = add
mix up = scramble together

16. pass out = lose consciousness
pass away = die

17. pick over = use your hands to isolate items thrown together, look at carefully
pick out = choose, select

18. put out = cause someone/something to go outside
put in = cause someone/something to go into a space

19. run into = meet unexpectedly
run for = become a candidate in an election
run up = increase (usually a bill)

20. stand for = support a policy/idea
stand out = be distinct

21. stay over = spend the night
stay up = remain awake longer than normal bed time

22. talk about = have a conversation with someone about someone else
talk to = have a conversation with someone

23. think up = imagine, create, pretend, make up
think over = consider, review
think about = reflect on, ponder, review

24. work out (+ object)/through = figure out/solve/resolve
work out (no object) = exercise

PHRASAL VERBS - WORKSHEET #2

Use the Phrasal Verb Chart to help you fill in the following blanks with the appropriate preposition or adverb. If you're not sure, check the meaning in a dictionary or www.dictionary.com

1. (act) After a game of Charades, in which they acted _________ an idea, a character from a story, or a song or movie title, the children began misbehaving and acting _________.

2. (break) After their car broke _________, the thieves broke _________ a house by breaking _________ a window.

3. (break) She decided to break _________ her engagement. Although she knew it was the right thing to do, she was sad about breaking _________.

4. (bring) The grandmother brought _________ all the photograph albums to show her grandchildren what a good job she had done in bringing _________ their father.

5. (burn) When he burned _________ the house, he also accidentally burned _________ the forest.

6. (call) After they had talked earlier, Jonathan called Patricia _________ in order to call _________ the wedding.

7. (carry) When her husband died, she had to carry _________ without him and try to carry _________ his wishes.

8. (cut) We need to cut _________ the red tape so we can cut _________ extra expense.

9. (dig) The Police Chief asked his detectives to dig _________ the files on the unsolved mystery and let him know what they dig _________.

10. (drop) I'll drop _________ your house after I drop my son _________ at his soccer practice.

11. (fill) Fill _________ the rental car application and then fill _________ the gas tank.

12. (hand) The teacher handed _________ the instructions and handed _________ the homework; then she asked the students to hand _________ the assignment that was due.

13. (iron) Planning the wedding became too complicated for the bride, so she hired someone to help her iron _________ all the details.

14.(let) Maggie let her friends __________ when she told them their clothes were too tight and they should let __________ the seams.

15. (pay) After the employer paid __________ all that money in bonuses, the employees were able to pay __________ some of their personal debt.

16. (pop) If an available appointment time pops __________, you can pop __________ and see the doctor.

17. (pull) The thieves casually pulled __________ the bank parking lot and were able to pull __________ a very successful robbery within five minutes.

18. (run) The other day when I ran __________ the grocery store to buy some eggs, the grocer told me they had run __________ .

19. (sign) The elderly man signed __________ the nursing home, and then he signed __________ his care to his daughter. He had earlier signed __________ all his property rights.

20. (slow) When the supervisor slowed the machine __________ , it also slowed __________ production.

21. (talk) We need to talk __________ the various options and then talk our boss __________ agreeing with our decision.

22. (take) I decided to take __________ the book about playing the guitar and decided to take __________ playing chess instead.

23. (throw) Throw __________ the fish, and throw __________ the bad food; otherwise, the smell will make me throw __________.

24. (wear) The effects of the medicine wore __________ by the time she returned home, but she was really worn __________ .

25. (write) Because you were in a car accident, you need to complete an accident report: write __________ a description of the accident, then write __________ all the information the report requires. The police will probably then write __________ a ticket.

SYNONYMS FOR PHRASAL VERBS - WORKSHEET #2

1. act out = portray another character, assume a role
    act up /out= misbehave

2. break down = (mechanical) become unable to use, malfunction
    (person) lose control, fall apart
    break into = force an entry into a space
    break through/out = force an entry through a particular opening

3. break off (+object) = end a relationship/partnership
    break up = end a relationship

4. bring out = gather/retrieve something in order to display/show
    bring up = raise/nurture children; introduce/raise an idea/opinion/suggestion to someone else

5. burn down = destroy from top to bottom/completely through fire
    burn up = destroy completely through fire

6. call back = return a phone call
    call off = cancel

7. carry on = continue
    carry out = fulfill, complete; transport something from one place to another in your arms/hands

8. cut through = quickly penetrate/expedite a series of requirements/policies
    cut out = eliminate

9. dig into = investigate/explore
    dig up = discover

10. drop by = come over for a quick visit
    drop off = take someone to someplace and leave them there

11. fill out/in = complete
    fill up = fill to capacity

12. hand out = distribute
    hand back = return by distributing something to someone
    hand in = give/return/turn in

13. iron out = smooth out/tackle/settle any difficulties or complications

14. let down = disappoint
    let out = make something larger by decreasing seam allowance

15. pay out = distribute money in expected/designated/pre-determined amounts
    pay off/back = satisfy/pay in full/completely
    pay down= reduce a bill or debt

16. pop up = appear
    pop over/in = make a short visit

17. pull into = ride/drive into a space to park
    pull off = accomplish/complete

18. run by = make a quick stop/visit
    run out = no longer have in stock

19. sign into = agree to reside in a hotel/hospital/facility
    sign over = legally give responsibility for something to someone for a certain length of time
    sign away = legally give up/relinquish any claim or rights to someone or something

20. slow down = reduce the speed of something/make slower
    slow up = lessen the output/reduce the speed of something/make slower

21. talk over/through = discuss
    talk into = influence

22. take back = return
    take up = begin a hobby/develop a skill

23. throw back = return
    throw away/out = dispose of/eliminate/discard
    throw up = vomit

24. wear off = diminish/fade/weaken
    wear out = exhaust/make tired/be drained of energy

25. write down = describe/put something on paper
    write in = provide information
    write out = complete/fill out

"Sorry to interrupt, but you've got subject-verb disagreement in the third stanza."

QUOTED SPEECH CHANGED TO REPORTED SPEECH

Adapted from Van Zante, Janis, Grammar Links 3, A Theme-Based Course for Reference and Practice, pp. 405-413, ©2005 Houghton Mifflin Co., Cengage Learning. Used with permission.

[….] = noun clauses following verbs that introduce reported speech.

QUOTED (Direct) SPEECH	REPORTED (Indirect) SPEECH

1. If the _verb that introduces the quote_ is in the present tense, there is _no change in the verb form of reported speech_:

- Michael says, "I **am** very angry with my girlfriend." Michael says [*that* he **is** very angry with his girlfriend].
- Karen always tells us, "Michael **will** never marry me." Karen tells us [*that* Michael **will** never marry her].

2. If the _verb that introduces the quote_ is in the past tense, the verb in reported speech changes form:

Simple Present changes to   **Simple Past**

- Betty said, "You **are** in love with Mary, not me." Betty said [*that* I **was** in love with Mary, not her].
- She said, "I **exercise** several times a week." She said [*that* she **exercised** several times a week].
- Emily asked Roberto, "Why do you **argue** with Maria?" Emily asked Roberto [*why* he argued with Maria].
- Emily asked Roberto, "Does Maria **love** you?" Emily asked Roberto [*if /whether* Maria **loved** him].

Present Progressive changes to   **Past Progressive**

- He announced, "I **am having** second thoughts." He announced [*that* he **was having** second thoughts].
- The pilot said, "We **are flying** over Mt. Fuji." The pilot said [*that* they **were flying** over Mt. Fuji].

Simple Past changes to   **Past Perfect**

- He replied, "I **wrote** her a letter last week." He replied [*that* he **had written** her a letter last week].

Past Progressive changes to   **Past Perfect Progressive**

- He declared, "We were discussing marriage." He declared [*that* they **had been discussing** marriage].

Present Perfect changes to   **Past Perfect**

- The agent demanded, "Where **have** you lived before?" The agent demanded (to know) [*where* I **had** lived before].

Present Perfect Progressive changes to   **Past Perfect Progressive**

- The student said, "I have been doing the best I can." The student said [*that* she had been doing the best she could].

3. *Some modals change forms in reported speech:*

Can* changes to** ⟶ ***Could

- I said, "He **can** try it."　　　　I said [*that* he **could** try it].
- The child asked, "**Can** I use the computer?"　　　　The child asked [if she **could** use the computer].

May* changes to** ⟶ ***Might

- Miriam told Carmen, "Carlos **may** be there now."　　　　Miriam told Carmen [*that* Carlos **might** be there now].

Will* changes to** ⟶ ***Would

- Carmen asked Miriam, "**Will** Carlos pick me up?"　　　　Carmen asked Miriam [if Carlos **would** pick her up].

Have to/Must* changes to** ⟶ ***Had to

- The student said, "I **have to** know the answer."　　　　The student said [*that* she **had** to know the answer].
- The policeman **told** me, "You must be quiet."　　　　The policeman **told** me [*that* I had to be quiet].

4. *No changes in reported speech if verbs are:*

- Past Perfect
- Present or Past *UNREAL* conditionals

5. <u>HOWEVER</u>, *all verb and modal changes mentioned above are <u>OPTIONAL</u> if reported speech:*

- expresses a general truth
- expresses a situation that is still true
- is about future events

6. *Other changes:*

- Subject, object and reflexive pronouns get changed if speaker(s) or listener(s) is/are not those of original speech
- Demonstrative pronouns get changed if not nearby in reported speech
- Time expressions get changed when the time of reported speech differs from original speech:

    Now ⟶ *then*
    Today ⟶ *that day, then*
    Tomorrow ⟶ *the next day*
    Yesterday ⟶ *the day before*
    Next week ⟶ *the following week*

- Place expressions

    Here ⟶ *there (or name of place)*
    there ⟶ *here (or name of place)*

PART II

WRITING

<u>THE AMAZING TWO-LETTER WORD "UP"</u>

There is one word in the English language that can be a noun, verb, adjective, adverb, and preposition: "**up**".

- It's easy to understand "**up**", meaning toward the sky or at the top of the list, but when we awaken in the morning, why do we <u>wake **up**</u>?

- A drain must be <u>opened **up**</u> because it is <u>clogged **up**</u>.

- When someone is telling the truth, we say he is <u>on the **up** and **up**</u>.

- The man who is <u>standing **up**</u> may not be an <u>**up**standing</u> citizen.

- To be dressed is one thing, but to be <u>dressed **up**</u> is special.

- We can say, "Sales are <u>on the **up**</u> this week" if they are increasing.

- People <u>stir **up**</u> trouble, <u>line **up**</u> for tickets, <u>work **up**</u> an appetite, and <u>think **up**</u> excuses.

- If the officers in an organization are <u>**up** for</u> election, and there is a tie, it is a <u>toss-**up**</u>.

- When a topic <u>comes **up**</u> at a meeting, we <u>speak **up**</u>; then, it is <u>**up** to</u> the secretary to <u>write **up**</u> a report about the meeting.

- We <u>call **up**</u> our friends, <u>brighten **up**</u> a room, <u>polish **up**</u> the silver, <u>warm **up**</u> the leftovers and <u>clean **up**</u> the kitchen. We <u>lock **up**</u> the house and <u>fix **up**</u> the old car.

- We <u>open **up**</u> a store in the morning; we <u>close it **up**</u> at night. We seem to be pretty <u>mixed **up**</u> about "**up**"!

- To be knowledgeable about the proper uses of "**up**", <u>look **up**</u> the word "**up**" in the dictionary. In a desk-sized dictionary, it <u>takes **up**</u> almost 1/4 of the page and can have <u>**up** to</u> thirty definitions.

- If you are <u>**up** to</u> it, you might try <u>building **up**</u> a list of the many ways "**up**" is used. It will <u>take **up**</u> a lot of your time, but if you don't <u>give **up**</u>, you may <u>wind **up**</u> with <u>**up** to</u> a hundred or more.

- When it threatens to rain, it is <u>clouding **up**</u>. When the sun comes out, it is <u>clearing **up**</u>. When we have rain, the earth <u>soaks it **up**</u>. When it does not rain for a while, things <u>dry **up**</u>.

- We could go on and on, but we should <u>wrap it **up**</u> for now. Our <u>time is **up**</u>.

BUILD A BRIDGE FOR YOUR READER

Transitions build bridges between ideas

showing the relationships between them

- Addition/Illustration
- Contrast/Comparison
- Reason/Result
- Time/Sequence

USING CONJUNCTIONS & CONNECTORS

Purpose	Coordinating Conjunctions	Sentence Connectors		Subordinating Conjunctions
ADDITION *ILLUSTRATION*	and but also nor not only	actually additionally also as a matter of fact as an example as well besides besides + N finally for example for instance for one thing	furthermore in addition in fact indeed in particular likewise moreover to illustrate too	
CONTRAST *COMPARISON*	and but yet	by comparison despite + N even so however in comparison in contrast in spite of + N instead instead of + N in the same way	likewise nevertheless nonetheless on the other hand in the same way on the contrary similarly still unlike + N	although despite the fact that even though in spite of the fact that just as though whereas while
REASON *RESULT*	for or (else) so	accordingly as a result as a result of + N as a consequence consequently for this reason hence In order to + V then therefore thus with this in mind		because if in order that providing that since so that unless
TIME *SEQUENCE*	and	above all after that eventually finally first first and foremost first of all last last of all more importantly most importantly	more significantly most significantly next now primarily shortly since then soon then	after as long as as soon as before once since until when whenever while

EITHER OR—NEITHER NOR

Either   or

1. Either the supervisor or the workers <u>are getting</u> a promotion this week.

2. Either the workers or the supervisor <u>is getting</u> a promotion this week.

3. Either rabbits or a turtle <u>eats</u> the lettuce in the garden.

4. Either a turtle or rabbits <u>eat</u> the lettuce in the garden.

5. Either the workers or the supervisor <u>has inspected</u> the construction site.

6. Either the supervisor or the workers <u>have inspected</u> the construction site.

WHEN USING "EITHER OR" AND "NEITHER NOR" IN A SENTENCE WITH BOTH A SINGULAR AND PLURAL SUBJECT, THE MAIN VERB MUST ALWAYS AGREE WITH THE SUBJECT CLOSEST TO IT.

Neither   or

1. Neither the rabbits nor the turtle ever <u>belongs</u> in the classroom.

2. Neither the turtle nor the rabbits ever <u>belong</u> in the classroom.

3. Neither the workers nor the supervisor <u>was being paid</u> over-time.

4. Neither the supervisor nor the workers <u>were being paid</u> over-time.

5. Neither the supervisor nor the workers <u>have gotten</u> a promotion this year.

6. Neither the workers nor the supervisor <u>has gotten</u> a promotion this year.

INTRODUCING EXAMPLES

"for example" *==> pay attention to the position and punctuation*:

1. Language influences perception. **For example,** the Eskimos have more than one word for "snow."

2. Language influences perception. The Eskimos, **for example,** have more than one word for "snow."

3. Language influences perception. The Eskimos have more than one word for "snow," **for example**.

4. Language influences perception; **for example,** the Eskimos have more than one word for "snow."

"for instance" *==> pay attention to the position and punctuation*:

1. Language influences perception. **For instance,** the Eskimos have more than one word for "snow."

2. Language influences perception. The Eskimos, **for instance,** have more than one word for "snow."

3. Language influences perception. The Eskimos have more than one word for "snow," **for instance**.

4. Language influences perception; **for instance,** the Eskimos have more than one word for "snow."

"like" *or* ***"such as"*** *==> these are interchangeable—no special punctuation*:

1. Job titles **such as** stewardess, waitress, and mailman are today considered sexist and have been replaced by non gender-specific job titles **like** flight attendant, server, and mail carrier.

2. Job titles **like** stewardess, waitress, and mailman are today considered sexist and have been replaced by non gender-specific job titles **such as** flight attendant, server, and mail carrier.

<u>THE COLON: WHAT DO YOU DO WITH THOSE DOUBLE DOTS?</u>

1. Use a colon after an independent clause to introduce a list, to rename the noun before it, or to introduce a quotation.

   ◊ We plan to visit all of the great tourist spots: the Garden of the Gods, Pikes Peak, and the Royal Gorge.

   ◊ She watched her favorite movie: *Gone with the Wind.*
   (using the colon here instead of a comma adds emphasis)

   ◊ Consider the words of George Elliott: "It's never to late to be who you might have been."

2. Use a colon between independent clauses if the second clause summarizes or explains the first.

   ◊ Faith is like love: it cannot be forced.

3. An independent clause <u>always</u> comes before a colon.

   ☹ Please bring: a sleeping bag, sturdy hiking shoes, and a flashlight.
   ☺ Please bring the following: a sleeping bag, sturdy hiking shoes, and a flashlight.

<u>PUNCTUATION CAN CHANGE YOUR LIFE!</u>

©Games Publications, Fort Washington, PA 19034; Gloria Rosenthal, <u>Games</u>, January, 1984; <u>games@kappapublishing.com</u>   Used with permission.

Dear John,

I want a man who knows what love is all about. You are generous, kind, thoughtful. People who are not like you admit to being useless and inferior. You have ruined me for other men. I yearn for you. I have no feelings whatsoever when we're apart. I can be forever happy-- will you let me be yours?

Gloria

Dear John,

I want a man who knows what love is. All about you are generous, kind, thoughtful people who are not like you. Admit to being useless and inferior. You have ruined me. For other men, I yearn. For you, I have no feelings whatsoever. When we're apart, I can be forever happy. Will you let me be?

Yours,

Gloria

Which letter would you like to receive?

PUNCTUATING CONJUNCTIONS & CONNECTORS

Coordinating Conjunctions	Sentence Connectors	Subordinate Conjunctions
These connect words, phrases, and clauses.	These connect independent clauses or paragraphs.	These connect *a dependent clause* to *an independent clause.*
Pay attention to:	Pay attention to:	Pay attention to:
• Purpose: *additive, contrast, cause/effect, sequence*	• Purpose: *addition, contrast, cause/effect, sequence*	• Purpose: *additive, contrast, cause/effect, sequence*
• Punctuation:	• Position: beginning, middle, or end	• Position: it determines punctuation
When connecting words *and* phrases:	• Punctuation	1. Introductory *Independent* Clause:
for / and / nor / but / or / yet / So	[Subject + Verb]; *sen con,* [Subject + Verb].	**[Subject + Verb]** *sub con* [Subject + Verb].
NO comma	[Subject + Verb]. *Sen Con,* [Subject + Verb].	**NO** comma
When connecting *independent clauses:*	[Subject + Verb]; [Subject, *+ sen con,* + Verb].	2. Introductory *Dependent* Clause:
[Subject + Verb], *for* [Subject + Verb]	[Subject + Verb]. [Subject, *+ sen con,* + Verb].	*Sub Con* [Subject + Verb], **[Subject + Verb].**
and / nor / boy / or / yet / so	[Subject + Verb]; [Subject + Verb, *sen con*].	<u>COMMA</u>
<u>COMMA</u>	[Subject + Verb]. [Subject + Verb, *sen con*].	
Practice Sentences	Practice Sentences	Practice Sentences
1.	1.	1.
2.	2.	2.
3.	3.	3.
4.	4.	4.

Even though we're stuck at the end of the sentence, we ARE important.
I am very sure about things. That's why I am always trying to get somebody's attention about something, even if I have to yell.
I'm not very sure about anything, so I am always asking a question.

PUNCTUATING TIME CLAUSES & PHRASES

Some of these time expressions introduce phrases, and others introduce clauses; there is specific punctuation for each use.

After / After that (refers to a previously mentioned time)
1. I started college *after* I had come to the United States.
   After I had come to the United States, <u>I started college</u>.

2. *After that*, I got married.
   I got married *after that.*

Before / Before that (refers to a previously mentioned time)
1. I had come to the United States *before* I started college.
   Before I started college, <u>I had come to the United States</u>.

2. *Before that*, I had lived in Switzerland.
   I had lived in Switzerland *before that*.

By / By the time / By that time (refers to a previously mentioned time)
1. *By* April, I will have had 12 teeth pulled.
   By 2025, I will have been in the US for 20 years.
   By 9:00 AM, I will have already had breakfast.

2. *By the time* I am 35 years old, I will have had 12 teeth pulled.
   I will have had 12 teeth pulled *by the time* I am 35 years old.

   By the time you make a decision, the problem will have disappeared.
   The problem will have disappeared *by the time* <u>you make a decision</u>.

3. *By that time,* we will have all lost our jobs.
   We will have all lost our jobs *by that time*.

<u>Until / Until then, Until that time</u> (both refer to a previously mentioned time)

1. *Until* we came to Colorado Springs, we had only spoken Russian.

   We had only spoken Russian *until* we came to Colorado Springs.

2. We had been studying Biology until last semester.

   Until last semester, <u>we had been studying Biology</u>.

3. We had been studying Geology *until then*.

   Until then, <u>we had been studying geology</u>.

4. We had been studying Geology *until that time.*

   Until that time, we had been studying Geology.

GOOD WRITING IS ABOUT QUALITY **NOT** QUANTITY

SUPPORTING YOUR ARGUMENT: INDUCTIVE/DEDUCTIVE REASONING

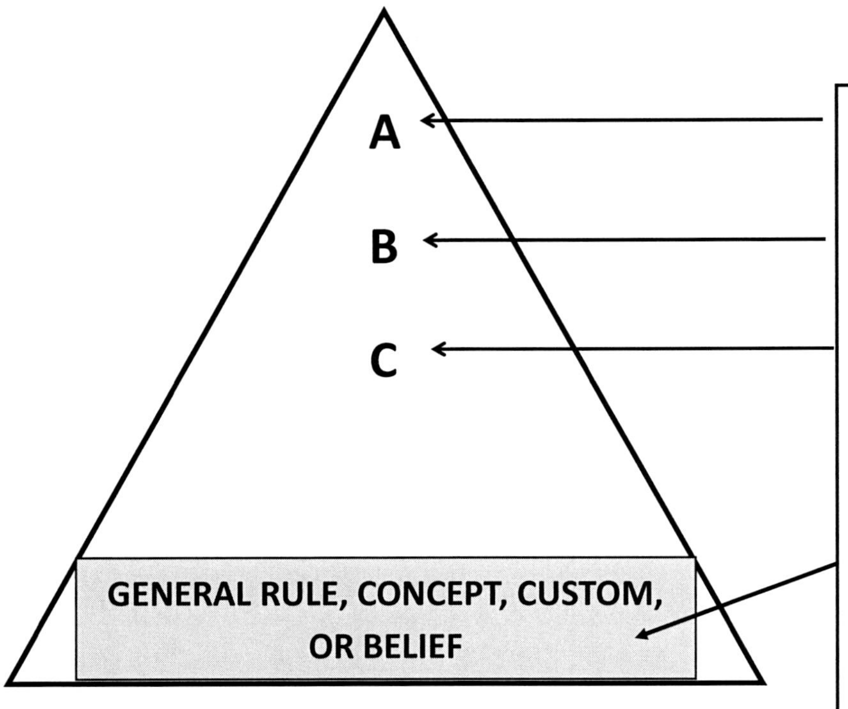

If **THIS** is observed or supposed to be true/right/wrong,

and **THIS** is observed or supposed to be true/right/wrong,

and **THIS** is observed or supposed to be true/right/wrong,

then they **lend support** for us to conclude **THIS**, even though this assumption or conclusion falls short of the absolute certainty of deductive arguments and the support may range from very strong to very weak.

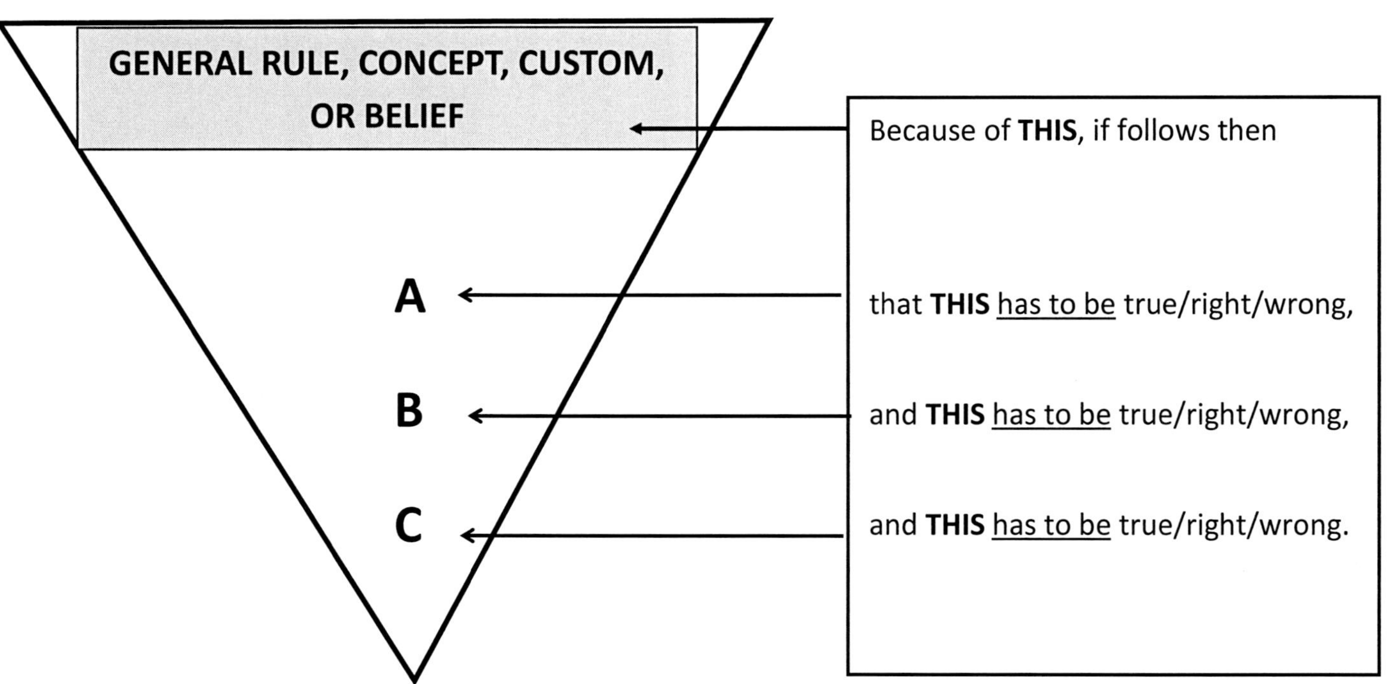

Because of **THIS**, if follows then

that **THIS** has to be true/right/wrong,

and **THIS** has to be true/right/wrong,

and **THIS** has to be true/right/wrong.

PART III

READING

<u>OWED TO MY SPELL CHECKER</u>

I have a grate spell checker;

It came with my PC.

It plainly Marx four my revue

Mistakes I cannot sea.

I've run this poem threw it,

And Yule be pleased to no

Its let her perfect in every weigh;

My checker toll me sew!

Credited to Mark Eckman, in "AT&T Today", 1991
by Richard Nordquist, grammar.about.com, and later altered and expanded into
"Candidate for a Pullet Surprise" by Jerrold H. Zar, for publication in the
Journal of Irreproducible Results in 1994: www.jir.com/pullet.html

IS IT AN "ABBREVIATION" OR AN "ACRONYM"?

Abbreviation		Acronym	
♦ An abbreviation is the shortened form of something, which can be a word or a phrase. For example, "St.", "Ave." and "Mt." stand for "saint", "avenue" and "mount". When you see these abbreviations, you pronounce the original word. Usually just the first letter is capitalized. ♦ However, you can also form abbreviations from the first letter of each word in a particular phrase. In these cases, you pronounce each letter like "F-B-I" or "U-S-A". "I. Q", for example, is the abbreviated form of "intelligence quotient". These are usually written in all capital letters.		♦ Like an abbreviation, you form an acronym from the first letters of a series of words in a phrase or the name of a particular group/organization. ♦ However, unlike an abbreviation, you most often pronounce an acronym as a word. You do not pronounce it letter by letter. ♦ An acronym is usually written in capital letters; however, once the acronym has been used in the language for a long time, only the first letter is capitalized (e.g. "Radar" or "Laser" or "Scuba").	
FBI	Federal Bureau of Investigation	NATO	North Atlantic Treaty Organization
UN	United Nations	AIDS	Acquired Immune Deficiency Syndrome
USA	United States of America	NASA	National Aeronautics & Space Administration
BBC	British Broadcasting Company	PETA	People for the Ethical Treatment of Animals
ABC	American Broadcasting Company	LASER	Light Amplification by Stimulated Emission of Radiation
NBC	National Broadcasting Company	SCUBA	Self-Contained Underwater Breathing Apparatus
CBS	Columbia Broadcasting System	RADAR	Radio Detection and Ranging
UK	United Kingdom	ASAP	As Soon As Possible (pronounced A-SAP)
PTA	Parents & Teachers Association	RAM	Random Access Memory
HTML	Hypertext Markup Language	POTUS	President of the United States
ASAP	As Soon As Possible	EDGAR	Electronic Data Gathering and Retrieval
WWW	World Wide Web	FedEx	Federal Express
TBA	To Be Announced	HUD	Department of Housing & Urban Development
USN	United States Navy		
PDA	Personal Digital Assistant		
FDA	Food & Drug Administration		
ICE	Immigration and Customs Enforcement		

THE BUILDING BLOCKS OF ENGLISH WORDS

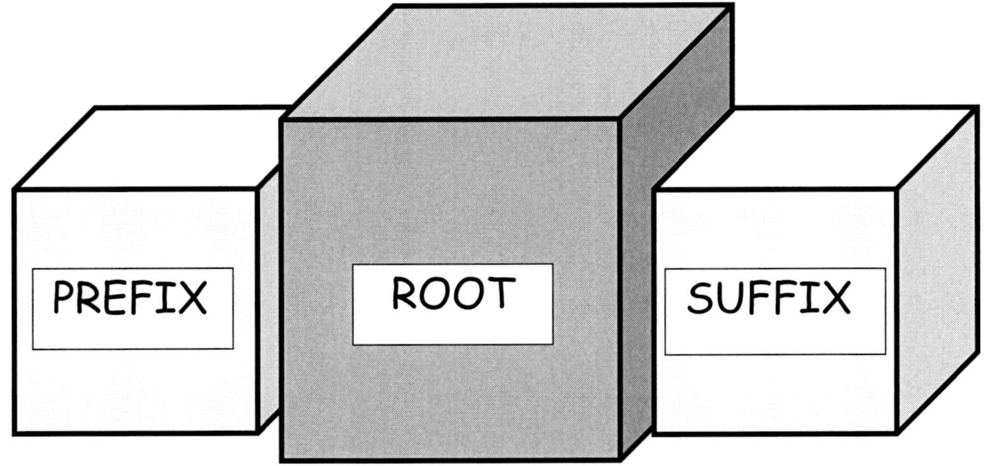

sub + mar + ine = *submarine*: "below water"

con + secut + ive = *consecutive*: "following in sequence with"

inter + ject + ion = *interjection*: "being thrown into"

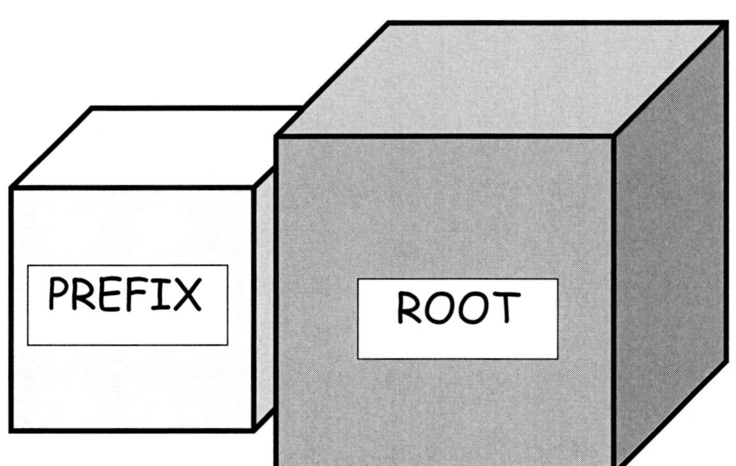

ad + mit = *admit*: "to send in"

bi + sect = *bisect*: "to cut in two"

circum + scrib = *circumscribe*: "to draw around"

pro + cede = *proceed*: "to go forward"

cred + ible = *credible*: "able to be believed"

ethn + ic = *ethnic*: "having the nature of a nation"

test + ify = *testify*: "to give witness"

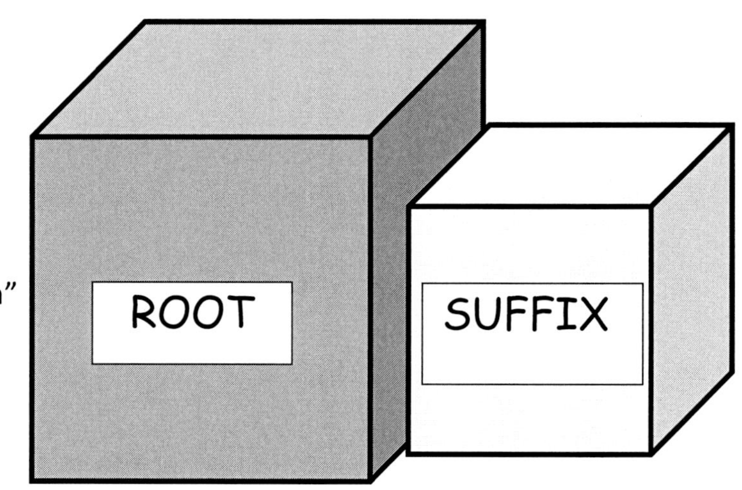

GREEK AND LATIN PREFIXES

BASE	MEANING	ORIGIN
a, ab	from, away	Latin
a, an	not	Greek
acro	top, tip, end	Greek
ad, ac, at, as, ap, am, an, ar, ag, af	to, toward, at	Latin
ambi	around, both	Latin
amphi	both, around	Greek
ana	back, opposite	Greek
ant, anti	against	Greek
ante	before	Latin
apo, ap, aph	away from, off	Greek
archa, arshae	old, ancient	Greek
auto	self	Greek
bene	good, well	Latin
bi	two	Latin
cent	hundred	Latin
circum	around	Latin
co, con, com, cor	together, with	Latin
contra, contro	against	Latin
de	from, away, off	Latin
deca, dec, deka	ten	Greek
di, dis	two, twice	Greek
dia	through, across, apart	Greek
dis, dif	apart, away, not, to deprive	Latin
du	double, two	Latin
dys	difficult, bad, ill	Greek
e, ex, ec	out, beyond, from, out of, forth	Latin
ecto	outside of	Greek
em, en	in, on	Greek
endo, ento	within	Greek
ep, epi	upon, at, in addition, on	Greek
eu	good, well	Greek
extra	beyond	Latin
fore	before	Anglo-Saxon

hemi	half	Greek
hepta	seven	Greek
hexa	six	Greek
hetero	various, unlike	Greek
hier	sacred	Greek
holo	whole	Greek
homo	same	Greek
hyper	above, beyond	Greek
hypo, hyp	under, less than	Greek
ideo, idea	idea	Greek
in, ir, im, il	not, without	Latin
in, im	in, on, upon, into, toward	Latin
inter	between, among	Latin
Intra	within, into	Latin
intro	within, into	Latin
iso	equal	Greek
kilo	thousand	Greek
macro	long, large	Greek
magn, mag, meg, maj	great	Latin
mal	bad, ill	Latin
mega	great	Greek
met, meta, meth	among, with, after, beyond	Greek
micro	small	Greek
migr	to move, travel	Latin
mill, mille	thousand	Latin
mis	less, wrong	Latin
mono	one	Greek
multi	many, much	Latin
neo	new	Greek
non, ne	not	Latin
nov	nine	Latin
o, ob, oc, of, op	against, toward, upon	Latin
oct	eight	Latin
omni	all	Latin
paleo	long ago, ancient	Greek
pan, panto	all, every	Greek
para	beside, beyond	Latin

penta	five	Greek
per	through	Latin
peri	around, about	Greek
poly	many	Greek
post	after	Latin
pre	before	Latin
pro	before, forward, forth	Latin
pronto	first	Greek
pseudo	false, counterfeit	Greek
quad, quatr	four	Latin
quint	five	Latin
re	again, anew, back	Latin
retro	back, backward, behind	Latin
se, sed	apart, aside, away	Latin
semi	half	Latin
sept	seven	Latin
sex	six	Latin
sover	above, over	Latin
sub	under, below, up from below	Latin
super, supra	above, down, more than	Latin
syn, sym, syl	together, with	Greek
tele	far off	Greek
tetra	four	Greek
trans	over, across	Latin
tri	three	Latin
ultra	beyond, extremely	Latin
un	not	Latin
uni	one	Latin

GREEK AND LATIN ROOTS

BASE	MEANING	ORIGIN
act	to act	Latin
acu, acr, ac	needle	Latin
acro	height, point	Greek
alt	high	Latin
alter	other	Latin
amor	love	Latin
andro	male	Greek
anima, anim	life, mind	Latin
ann, anno, enn	year	Latin
anthropo	mankind	Greek
aqua	water	Latin
arch, archi	govern, rule, chief	Greek
arm	army, weapon	Latin
arbitr, arbiter	to judge, consider	Latin
art	craft, skill	Latin
arthr, art	segment, joint	Greek
aster, astro	star	Greek
aud, audio	to hear, sound	Latin
bell	war	Latin
biblio, bibl	book	Greek
bio	life	Greek
brev	short	Latin
capit, cipit, caput	head	Latin
capt	take, hold	Latin
carn	flesh	Latin
caus	cause, case, lawsuit	Latin
ced, cede	to go, yield	Latin
cele	honor	Latin
cell	to rise, project	Latin
cent	one hundred	Latin
cept, capt, cip, cap, ceive, ceipt	to take, hold, grasp	Latin
cert	sure, to trust	Latin
cess, ced	to move, withdraw	Latin
chrom	color	Greek

chron	time	Greek
cid, cide, cis	to cut off, be brief, to kill	Latin
circ, circum	around	Latin
cite	speak, say, tell, call	Latin
civ, civis	citizen	Latin
clar	clear	Latin
claud	close, shut, block	Latin
clin	to lean, lie, bend	Latin
cog	to know	Latin
column	a column	Latin
comput	to compute	Latin
cont	to join, unite	Latin
cor, cord, cour, card	heart	Latin
corp	body	Latin
cosm	world, order, universe	Greek
crac, crat, cracy	rule, govern	Greek
cred	believe, trust	Latin
crit, cris	separate, discern, judge	Latin
crypt	hidden, secret	Greek
culp	fault, blame	Latin
curs, curr, corr	to run	Latin
custom	one's own	Latin
cycl	circle	Greek
dem	people	Greek
dent, odon	tooth	Latin
derm	skin	Greek
dic, dict	to say, to speak, assert	Latin
duct, duc	to lead, draw	Latin
dur	to harden, hold out	Latin
dyna	power	Greek
ego	"I"	Latin
ethn	nation	Greek
equ	equal, fair	Latin
fac, fic, fect, fact	to make, to do	Latin
famil	Family	Latin
fen	to strike	Latin
fer	to carry, bear, bring	Latin

fid	trust, faith	Latin
fin	to end	Latin
flu	to flow	Latin
form	shape, form	Latin
fort	chance, luck, strong	Latin
frat	brother	Latin
frig	cool	Latin
fum	smoke, scent	Latin
gam	marriage	Greek
gen	race, birth, kind	Latin
geo	earth	Greek
gnos	know, knowledge	Greek
grad	walk, step, go	Latin
gram, graph	write, written	Greek
gress	walk, step, go	Latin
gyn	female	Greek
hetereo	different	Greek
homo	same	Greek
hydr	water	Greek
ject	throw	Latin
junct	join	Latin
juris	right, justice, law	Latin
jus	right, justice, law	Latin
loc	place	Latin
locu, loqu	speak	Latin
log	speech, speak	Greek
luc	light	Latin
magn	great	Latin
man	hand	Latin
mania	madness	Latin
mar, mari, mer	sea, pool	Latin
mater	mother	Latin
medi	middle	Greek
mega	large, great	Latin
ment	mind	Greek
meter, metr	measure	Greek
mim	copy, imitate	Greek
mis	hate, hatred	

mit, miss	to send	Latin
mor	fool, manner, custom	Greek
morph	form	Greek
mort	death	Latin
mov, mob, mot	to move	Latin
mus	little mouse	Latin
mut	change, exchange	Latin
nat	birth, born	Latin
necess	unavoidable	Latin
neur, nerv	nerve	Greek
noc, nox	night, harm	Latin
nom, nomen, nomin,	name	Latin
null, nihil, nil	nothing, void	Latin
nym, onym, onom	name	Greek
ocul	eye	Latin
ology	study of	Greek
opt	eye	Greek
ord, ordin	order	Latin
ortho	straight, corrective	Greek
osteo	bone	Latin
pac, pax	peace	Latin
pan	all	Greek
par, pair	arrange, prepare, get ready, set	Latin
par, part, pars	equal, portion, part	Latin
pater	father	Latin
path	feeling, suffering, disease	Greek
ped, pes	foot	Latin
pel	drive	Latin
pend, pond, pens	to weigh, pay, consider	Latin
phe, fa, fe	speak, spoken about	Greek
phil	love	Greek
phobe	fear	Greek
phon	sound, voice	Greek
photo	light	Greek
plen	full	Latin
plet	fill	Latin
plic	to fold	Latin

plur, plus	more	Latin
pneu	breath	Greek
pod	foot, feet	Greek
polis, polit	citizen, city, state	Greek
pon	place, put	Latin
popul	people	Latin
port	to carry	Latin
pos	to place, put	Latin
pot	powerful	Latin
prim, prin	first	Latin
priv	separate	Latin
prob	to prove, test	Latin
pseudo	false, fake	Greek
psych	mind, soul, spirit	Greek
pyr	fire	Greek
reg, rig, rect, reign	government, rule, right, straight	Latin
respond	to answer	Latin
rupt	break, burst	Latin
sacr, secr, sacer	sacred	Latin
sat	to please, enough	Latin
sci	to know	Latin
scope	to see	Greek
scrib, script	to write	Latin
sect	cut	Latin
sed, sid, sess	to sit, to settle	Latin
sen	old	Latin
sent, sens	to feel	Latin
sequ, secut	to follow, sequence	Latin
sign	mark, sign	Latin
simil, simul, sembl	together, likeness, pretense	Latin
sol, soli	alone, lonely	Latin
solus	to comfort, to console	Latin
somn	sleep	Latin
son	sound	Latin
soph	wise	Greek
soror	sister	Latin
spec, spect, spic	to look at, behold	Latin

spir	breathe	Latin
spond, spons	to pledge, promise	Latin
stat	stand	Latin
strict	tighten	Latin
tac, tic	silent	Latin
tact	touch	Latin
techn	art, skill	Greek
tele	far, distant	Greek
temp	time	Latin
ten, tain, tent	to hold	Latin
tend, tens	to give heed, stretch toward	Latin
term, termin	boundary, limit	Latin
terra	earth, land	Latin
test	to witness, affirm	Latin
the, them, thet	to place, put	Greek
theatr	to see, view	Greek
theo	god	Greek
therm	heat, warm	Greek
tom, tomy	cut	Greek
topo	place	Greek
tort	twist	Latin
tract	to pull, draw	Latin
trib	to allot, give	Latin
vac	empty	Latin
ven	to come	Latin
ver	truth	Latin
vers, vert	to turn	Latin
vest	to adorn	Latin
vestig	to track	Latin
via	way, road	Latin
vir	manliness, worth	Latin
vis, vid	to see, to look	Latin
viv, vit	life	Latin
voc, vok	voice, call	Latin
vol	wish	Latin
zo, zoo	animal	Greek

GREEK AND LATIN SUFFIXES (and others)

Noun-forming suffixes

SUFFIX	MEANING	ORIGIN
age	belongs to	Latin
ance	state of being	Latin
ancy	state of, act of	Latin
ant	thing or person who	Latin
ar	relating to, like	Latin
arium	a place for	—————
ate	a person who	Latin
ation	action	Latin
ary	relating to, like	Latin
dom	state of	Old English
ee, eer, er	a person who	Old English
ence, ency	state of, fact, quality of	Latin
ent	a person who	Latin
ery	a place for	Middle English
hood	a state of	Old English / German
ice	state of	—————
ier	a person who	Old French / Latin
ion, tion, ation	being, the result of	Latin
ism	act of, practice of	Latin / Greek
ist	a person who	Latin
ity	state of, condition of	Middle English / Latin
ive	belonging to, quality of	Latin
ment	a means, product, act of, state of	Latin
mony	condition of, state of	—————
ness	state of, condition of	Old English / German
oid	like	Latin / Greek
or	a person or thing that	Latin
ory	relating to, like	Latin
osis	condition of, state of	Latin
ship	state of, condition of	Old English / French
sis	process of, state of	Latin /Greek
tion	act of, process of	Latin

tude	state of, quality of	Latin / French
try	profession, art of	————-
ty	condition of, quality of	Latin
ure	act of	Latin / French
y	creates abstract noun	Greek / Anglo-Saxon

Adjective-forming suffixes

SUFFIX	MEANING	ORIGIN
able	capable of being	Latin
ac	like, related to	—————
acious	having the quality	Latin
al	like, suitable for, related to	Latin
an	belonging to	Latin /French
ant	thing or person who	Latin
acy	quality of, state of	—————
ar	relating to, like	Latin
ary	relating to, like	Latin
ate	to become associated with	Latin
ern	relating to	—————
ese	relating to	Latin / French
esque	in the style of	Old French
ful	full of	Old English
ial	function of	Latin
ian	belonging to	Latin / French
ible	capable of being	Latin
ic	like, having the nature of	Latin / Greek
ile, ine	like, having the nature of, a feminine ending	Latin / French
ical	like	Middle English / Latin
ine	nature of; eminine ending	Latin
itis	inflammation	Latin / Greek
ive	belonging to, quality of	Latin
lent	full of	—————
less	without	Old English / Old Norse
ory	place for	Latin
ous	characterized by, having quality of	Latin

some	like	Old English / Old Norse
ulent	full of	Latin
y	quality, somewhat like	Greek /Anglo-Saxon

Verb-forming suffixes

SUFFIX	MEANING	ORIGIN
ate	to become associated with	Latin
en	to make, become	Middle English
fy, ify	make, do	Latin
ise, ize	to become like	Latin

Adverb-forming suffixes

SUFFIX	MEANING	ORIGIN
ic	like, having the nature of	Latin / Greek
ly	like, to extent of	Latin

PART IV

PRONUNCIATION

THIS IS DRIVING ME CRAZY!

©SH Chambers; www.shchambers.com Used with permission.

ESSENTIALS OF INTELLIGIBLE SPEECH

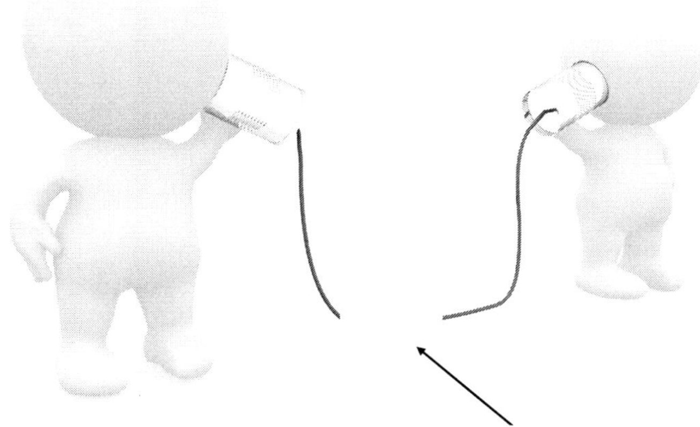

What creates a disconnect for you even if you are speaking English?

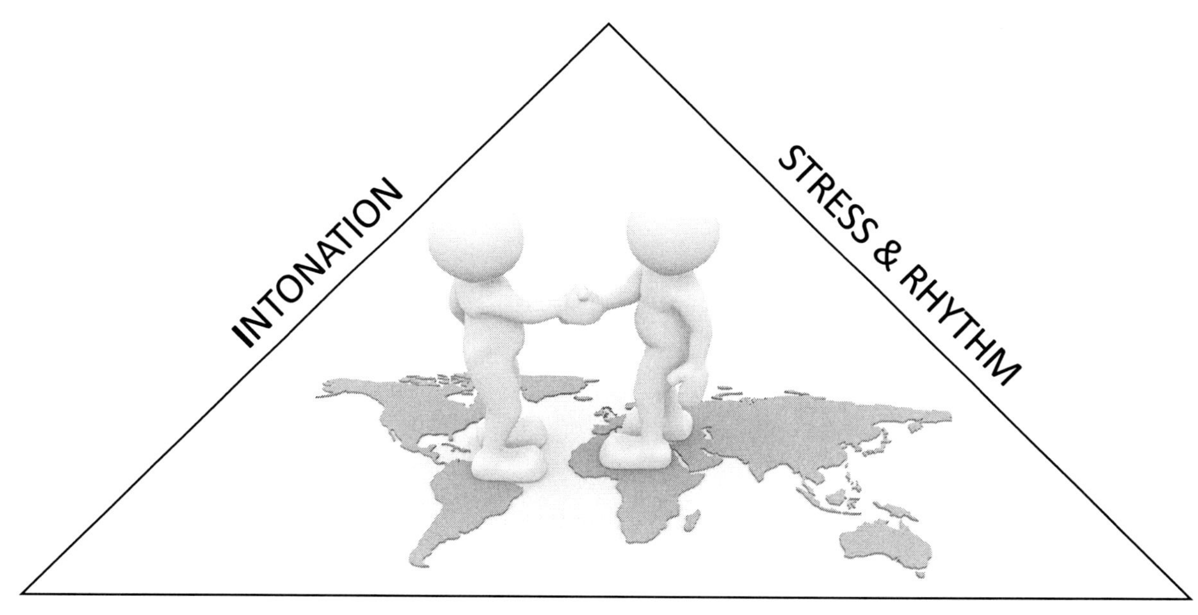

Unfortunately, smooth cross-cultural communication doesn't always happen just because you know the grammar and vocabulary of English well. You will connect much more easily as a listener and speaker if you learn the common patterns of intonation, stress/rhythm, and pronunciation in English.

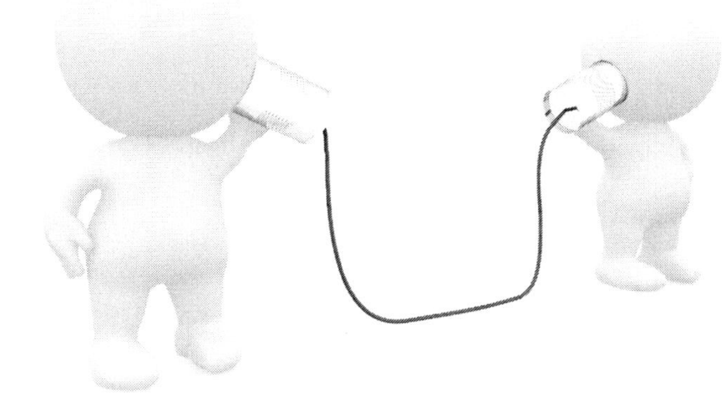

Whose Is This Anyway?

1. A. Whose is this? Is it yours or his?

/z/ɪz/ /s/ /ɪzɪt/ /z/ /z/
Whose is this? Is it yours or his?

2. B. It's his.

/s/ /z/
It's his.

3. A. It is? No, I'm sure it's yours.

/ɪtɪz/ /ɪts/ /z/
It is? No, I'm sure it's yours.

4. B. It's not mine. Maybe it's hers.

/ɪts/ /ɪts/ /z/
It's not mine. Maybe it's hers.

5. A. Hers? It's not yours?

/z/ /ɪts/ /z/
Hers? It's not yours?

6. B. No, I think it's hers.

/ɪts/ /z/
No, I think it's hers.

7. A. It could be hers or theirs.

/z/ /z/
It could be hers or theirs.

8. B. Theirs, but not ours.

/z/ /z/
Theirs, but not ours.

9. Ours is there. Theirs is here.

/zɪz/ /zɪz/
Ours is there. Theirs is here.

10. A. But they're not here. They're there.

But they're not here. They're there.

11. B. Then, it's theirs.

/s/ /z/
Then, it's theirs.

12. A. Whose is this anyway?

/zɪz/ /s/
Whose is this anyway?

PRONUNCIATION = SOUND PRODUCTION

1. involves position of lips, tongue, teeth, jaw

   - Can be difficult because of using new muscles
   - Familiar sounds in unfamiliar positions: initial, medial, final
   - Unfamiliar sounds
   - Air: voiced or voiceless

2. pronunciation can be complicated even more by

   - the spelling of certain sounds
   - the same spelling of different sounds
   - the different spelling of same sounds

How do you think "g‑h‑o‑t‑i" is pronounced?

Answer is on the back ⟶

"g–h–o–t–i" is pronounced "fish"**

How can that be?

<gh> = /f/ as in "cou_gh_"*
<o> = /ɪ/ as in "w_o_men"*
<ti> = /ʃ/ as in "vaca_ti_on"*
F-I-SH

*Sounds are rendered in IPA

This illustrates the frustrating mismatch between English spelling and pronunciation.

** Credited to William Ollier, Jr., a spelling reformer in 1855

IPA PRONUNCIATION GUIDE

Vowel Sounds	
*We **show** the sound this way:*	*We can **spell** the sound this way (underlined letters)*
1. /i/ /iy/	b<u>ea</u>t, f<u>ee</u>d
2. /ɪ/	b<u>i</u>t, k<u>i</u>ck
3. /eɪ/ /ey/	d<u>a</u>te, pl<u>ai</u>n
4. /ɛ/	b<u>e</u>t, d<u>e</u>bt
5. /æ/	b<u>a</u>t, l<u>a</u>p
6. /a/	f<u>a</u>ther, b<u>o</u>ther
7. /ə/ /ʌ/**	<u>u</u>p, c<u>u</u>t, sod<u>a</u>
8. /ɔ/	b<u>ou</u>ght, d<u>o</u>g
9. /oʊ/ /ow/	b<u>oa</u>t, t<u>o</u>te
10. /ʊ/	b<u>oo</u>k, g<u>oo</u>d
11. /u/ /uw/	b<u>oo</u>t, st<u>u</u>dent
12. /ɚ/ /ər/	sh<u>ir</u>t, m<u>ur</u>der
13. /aɪ/ /ay/	b<u>i</u>te, cr<u>y</u>, b<u>uy</u>
14. /aʊ/ /aw/	ab<u>ou</u>t, h<u>ow</u>
15. /ɔɪ/ /oy/	v<u>oi</u>ce, b<u>oy</u>,
16. /ɪr/ /ɪɚ/	b<u>ee</u>r, p<u>ie</u>r, f<u>ea</u>r
17. /ɛɪ/ /ɛɚ/	b<u>are</u>, b<u>ear</u>, h<u>air</u>
18. /ar/ /aɚ/	<u>are</u>, b<u>ar</u>, guit<u>ar</u>
19. /ɔr/ /ɔɚ/	d<u>oor</u>, f<u>our</u>
20. /ʊr/ /ʊɚ/	t<u>our</u>, s<u>ure</u>
21. /aɪɚ/	<u>iron</u>, f<u>ire</u>, ret<u>ired</u>
22. /aʊɚ/	<u>our</u>, h<u>our</u>, fl<u>ower</u>

Consonant Sounds	
*We **show** the sound this way:*	*We can **spell** the sound this way (underlined letters)*
1. /p/	<u>p</u>ack, ha<u>pp</u>y
2. /b/	<u>b</u>ack, ru<u>bb</u>er
3. /t/	<u>t</u>ie, bu<u>tt</u>on, wash<u>ed</u>
4. /d/	<u>d</u>ie, bu<u>tt</u>er, frie<u>d</u>
5. /k/	<u>c</u>ame, <u>k</u>ey, <u>q</u>uick
6. /g/	<u>g</u>ame, <u>g</u>uest
7. /tʃ/	<u>ch</u>urch, na<u>t</u>ure, wa<u>tch</u>
8. /dʒ/	<u>j</u>udge, <u>g</u>eneral, ma<u>j</u>or
9. /f/	<u>f</u>an, <u>ph</u>otogra<u>ph</u>, lau<u>gh</u>
10. /v/	<u>v</u>an, o<u>f</u>, wa<u>v</u>e
11. /θ/	<u>th</u>ing, brea<u>th</u>,
12. /ð/	brea<u>the</u>, <u>th</u>en, fea<u>th</u>er
13. /s/	<u>s</u>ip, <u>c</u>ity, p<u>s</u>ychology
14. /z/	<u>z</u>ip, plea<u>s</u>e, goe<u>s</u>
15. /ʃ/	<u>sh</u>ip, ma<u>ch</u>ine, sta<u>ti</u>on
16. /ʒ/	mea<u>s</u>ure, vi<u>s</u>ion
17. /h/	<u>h</u>ot, <u>wh</u>o
18. /m/	<u>m</u>en, su<u>mm</u>er, la<u>mb</u>
19. /n/	su<u>n</u>, <u>kn</u>ow, <u>pn</u>eumonia
20. /ŋ/	su<u>ng</u>, ri<u>ng</u>ing
21. /w/ /hw/	<u>w</u>et, <u>wh</u>ile
22. /l/	<u>l</u>ight, whi<u>l</u>e
23. /r/	<u>r</u>ight, <u>wr</u>ong
24. /y/	<u>y</u>es, <u>u</u>se, m<u>u</u>sic

**/ə/ (unstressed) /ʌ/ (stressed)

COMMON PRONUNCIATION KEYS

VOWEL SOUNDS				CONSONANT SOUNDS			
	Common Dictionary Keys	IPA	Spelling		Common Dictionary Keys	IPA	Spelling
1.	ē, ii, i:	/i/ /iy/	beat, feed	1.	p	/p/	pack, happy
2.	ĭ	/ɪ/	bit, women	2.	b	/b/	back, rubber
3.	ā	/eɪ/ /ey/	date	3.	t	/t/	tie, button, washed
4.	ĕ	/ɛ/	bet	4.	d	/d/	die, butter, fried
5.	ă	/æ/	bat	5.	k	/k/	came, key, quick
6.	ä, ŏ	/a/	father	6.	g	/g/	game, guest
7.	ŭ	/ə/ /ʌ/	up, cut, soda	7.	ch, č	/tʃ/	church, nature, watch
8.	ô	/ɔ/	bought, dog	8.	j, dž	/dʒ/	judge, general, major
9.	ō	/oʊ/ /ow/ /o/	boat	9.	f	/f/	fan, photograph, laugh
10.	oŏ	/ʊ/	book, good	10.	v	/v/	van
11.	oō, uu, u:	/u/ /uw/	boot, student	11.	th	/θ/	thing, breath
12.	ŭr, ər	/ɚ/ /ər/	shirt, murder	12.	*th*	/ð/	breathe, then
13.	ī	/aɪ/ /ay/	bite, cry, buy	13.	s	/s/	sip, city, psychology
14.	ou	/aʊ/ /aw/	about, how	14.	z	/z/	zip, please, goes
15.	oi	/ɔɪ/ /ɔy/	voice, boy,	15.	sh, š	/ʃ/	ship, machine, station, special
16.	îr	/ɪr/ /ɪɚ/	beer, fear	16.	zh, ž	/ʒ/	measure, vision
17.	âr	/ɛr/ /ɛɚ/	bare, bear	17.	h	/h/	hot, who
18.	är	/ar/ /aɚ/	are, bar, guitar	18.	m	/m/	men, summer, lamb
19.	ôr	/ɔr/ /ɔɚ/	door, four	19.	n	/n/	sun, know, pneumonia
20.	oŏr	/ʊr/ /ʊɚ/	tour, sure	20.	ng	/ŋ/	sung, ringing
21.	īr	/aɪɚ/	iron, fire, retired	21.	hw, w	/w/ hw/	wet, while
22.	our	/aʊɚ/	our, hour, flower	22.	l	/l/	light, while
				23.	r	/r/	right, wrong
				24.	y	/y/	yes, use, music

PRONUNCIATION OF VERBS WITH ADDED <-ed> OR <d>

(sounds shown in International Phonetic Alphabet)

- simple past tense form of regular verbs

<ed> = /t/ 1) after words ending in these sounds: /p, k, f, θ, s, ʃ, tʃ/		<ed> = /d/ 1) after words ending in these sounds: /b, g, v, ð, z, ʒ, dʒ, m, n, ŋ, l, r/ 2) or all vowel sounds		<ed> = /ɪd/ 1) after words ending in these sounds: /d, t/ 2) or ending in these letters: <d, dd, de, t, tt, te>	
Ask	*asked*	Grab	*grabbed*	Depart	*departed*
Divorce	*divorced*	Tug	*tugged*	Explode	*exploded*
Face	*faced*	Love	*loved*	Need	*needed*
Hop	*hopped*	Breathe	*breathed*	Separate	*separated*
Laugh	*laughed*	Change	*changed*	Start	*started*
Watch	*watched*	Close	*closed*	Visit	*visited*
		Gaze	*gazed*	Want	*wanted*
		Judge	*judged*		
		Frame	*framed*		
		Open	*opened*		
		Marry	*married*		
		Peel	*peeled*		
		Study	*studied*		
		Bother	*bothered*		
		Matter	*mattered*		

PRONUNCIATION OF WORDS WITH ADDED <s>, <es>, OR <'s>

(sounds shown in International Phonetic Alphabet)

- Verbs in 3rd person singular
- Plural nouns
- Possessives (plural possessives not shown)

<s>, <es>, <'s> = /s/ 1) after words ending in these sounds: /p, t, k, f, θ/				<s>, <es>, <'s> = /z/ 1) after words ending in these sounds: /b, d, g, v, ð, m, n, ŋ, l, r / 2) or after all vowel sounds				<s>, <es>, <'s> = /ɪz/ 1) after words ending in these sounds: / s, z, ʃ, ʒ, tʃ, dʒ / 2) or ending in these letters: < s, ss, se, z, zz, ze, sh, ch, tch, ge, ce, x >			
Nouns Verbs	3rd person singular	plural	possessive	Nouns Verbs	3rd person singular	plural	possessive	Nouns Verbs	3rd person singular	plural	possessive
Ask	*asks*			Breathe	*breathes*			Face	*faces*	*faces*	*face's*
Cut	*cuts*	*cuts*	*cut's*	Buy	*buys*			Fix	*fixes*	*fixes*	
Fight	*fights*	*fights*	*fight's*	Cover	*covers*	*covers*	*cover's*	Close	*closes*		
Hop	*hops*	*hops*	*hop's*	Decide	*decides*			Gaze	*gazes*	*gazes*	*gaze's*
Laugh	*laughs*	*laughs*	*laugh's*	Dream	*dreams*	*dreams*	*dream's*	Judge	*judges*	*judges*	*judge's*
Shop	*shops*	*shops*	*shop's*	Enjoy	*enjoys*			Notice	*notices*	*notices*	*notice's*
Take	*takes*			Feel	*feels*			Wash	*washes*	*washes*	*wash's*
Think	*thinks*			Love	*loves*			Watch	*watches*	*watches*	*watch's*
Want	*wants*			Say	*says*						
Breath		*breaths*	*breath's*	Sign	*signs*	*signs*	*sign's*				
				Sing	*sings*						
				Tug	*tugs*	*tugs*	*tug's*				

PRACTICE WITH "TH" /θ/, /ð/

INITIAL		MEDIAL		FINAL	
than	/ð/	bathtub	/θ/	bath	/θ/
thank	//θ/	bother	/ð/	both	/θ/
that	/ð/	brother	/ð/	breath	/θ/
the	/ð/	either	/ð/	breathe	/ð/
theater	/θ/	father	/ð/	broth	/θ/
theft	/θ/	feather	/ð/	death	/θ/
their	/ð/	healthy	/θ/	depth	/θ/
them	/ð/	mathematics	/θ/	earth	/θ/
themselves	/ð/	mother	/ð/	eighteenth	/θ/
then	/ð/	neither	/ð/	eighth	/θ/
therapy	/θ/	northern	/ð/	eleventh	/θ/
there	/ð/	other	/ð/	faith	/θ/
therefore	/ð/	rather	/ð/	fifteenth	/θ/
thermometer	/θ/	rhythm	/ð/	fifth	/θ/
thermostat	/θ/	southern	/ð/	fourteenth	/θ/
these	/ð/	truthful	/θ/	fourth	/θ/
they're	/ð/	weather	/ð/	moth	/θ/
thick	/θ/	youthful	/θ/	mouth	/θ/
thicker	/θ/			nineteenth	/θ/
thief	/θ/			ninth	/θ/
thigh	/θ/			north	/θ/
thin	/θ/			seventeenth	/θ/
thing	/θ/			seventh	/θ/
think	/θ/			sixteenth	/θ/
third	//θ/			sixth	/θ/
thirsty	/θ/			south	/θ/
thirteenth	/θ/			strength	/θ/
thirty	/θ/			tenth	/θ/
thirty-three	/θ/			thirteenth	/θ/
this	/ð/			thirtieth	/θ/
those	/ð/			tooth	/θ/
thought	/θ/			truth	/θ/
three	/θ/			twelfth	/θ/
throat	/θ/			underneath	/θ/
throw/threw	/θ/			wealth	/θ/
thumb	/θ/			width	/θ/
thunder	/θ/			with	/θ/
				youth	/θ/

© MARK ANDERSON
WWW.ANDERTOONS.COM
"What's another word for synonym?"

INTONATION: STATEMENTS & QUESTIONS

<u>Statement</u>: intonation rises and then falls on last stressed word or syllable

1. He went to the bookstore.

2. She likes that young man.

3. This class should help your pronunciation.

<u>Information Question</u>:   intonation falls on the last stressed word or syllable.

1. What time is the party?

2. How much is tuition?

3. When did she go to the store?

<u>Yes – No Question</u>: intonation rises on the last stressed word or syllable

1. Is the party at 6:00?

2. Did he come home on Tuesday?

INTONATION: "TAG" QUESTIONS

1. It's hot, isn't it?
2. You work at Memorial Hospital, don't you?
3. She's a wonderful nurse, isn't she?
4. You can climb Pikes Peak, can't you?
5. You didn't go to work yesterday, did you?
6. He isn't the manager, is he?
7. You aren't coming to the party, are you?
8. You don't like Mexican food, do you?

The **tag** has rising intonation if speaker is **NOT SURE** listener agrees.

+	-	-	+
(affirmative) statement	(negative) tag	(negative) statement	(affirmative) tag
1. It's hot,	isn't it?	5. You didn't go to work yesterday,	did you?
2. You work at Memorial Hospital,	don't you?	6. He isn't the manager,	is he?
3. She's a wonderful nurse,	isn't she?	7. You aren't coming to the party,	are you?
4. You can climb Pikes Peak,	can't you?	8. You don't like Mexican food,	do you?

The **tag** has falling intonation if speaker is **SURE** listener agrees.

Statement always has falling intonation.

<u>STRESS & RHYTHM: THE MUSIC AND MEANING OF ENGLISH</u>

THE "MUSIC AND MEANING" OF ENGLISH IS CREATED BY:

1. <u>WORD STRESS</u>

   - The stressed syllable in multi-syllable words is not consistent.

     - ma**CHINE**, **HAM**mer

     - edu**CA**tion, bi**O**logy, **WA**termelon

2. <u>SENTENCE STRESS</u>

   - English (and German) are **"stress-timed"** languages.

     - Some syllables take longer to say than others, so the time it takes to say something does not depend on the number of syllables.

       ⇒ duh-**DUH**-duh-**DUUUH**-duh*

     - Content words **are stressed**; this creates a "beat".

       ⇒ Nouns: *kitchen, Peter*

       ⇒ (most) main verbs: *visit, eat*

       ⇒ Adjectives: *beautiful, interesting*

       ⇒ Adverbs: *often, carefully*

     - Function words are either **NOT stressed,** or they are reduced.

       ⇒ Determiners: *the, a, some, a few*

       ⇒ Auxiliary verbs: *don't, am, can, were, could*

       ⇒ Prepositions: *before, next to, opposite*

       ⇒ Conjunctions: *but, while, as*

       ⇒ Pronouns: *they, she, us*

     - Misplaced stress throws the listener off.

   - Spanish, French, Italian, Brazilian Portuguese, and some Chinese dialects are **"syllable-timed"** languages.

- Most syllables take the same length of time to say, so the time it takes to say something depends on the number of syllables.

  ⇒ duh-duh-duh-duh-duh-duh*

- If your native language is syllable-timed, you might struggle with the stress and rhythm of English sentences.

I want to go to the store after work to buy milk.

- Neutral sentence stress: sharing information

- Stressed words receive higher pitch

- Pitch also rises and then falls on last stressed word or syllable

Listen to the music of English:

I want to <u>go</u> to the <u>store</u>.
I want to <u>go</u> to the <u>store</u> after <u>work</u>.
I want to <u>go</u> to the <u>store</u> after <u>work</u> to buy <u>milk</u>.

We cram our unstressed words together, in between the stressed words, in such a way that the stressed words occur more or less on a beat at regular time intervals . . . like music.

*Mary Peacock, Xans World, www.youtube.com/watch?v=sUMM5eCvi8w, 1/24/2010

"THE STORY OF ESAU WOOD"

"The Story of Esau Wood" is a famous Tongue Twister, which acting classes frequently use to teach the importance of stress, rhythm, and intonation. Although this story is grammatically correct, it is very confusing and seems to have no meaning, especially when we try to read it like this:

Esau Wood sawed wood. Esau Wood would saw wood. All the wood Esau Wood saw, Esau Wood would saw. In other words, all the wood Esau saw to saw, Esau sought to saw. Oh, the wood Wood would saw! And oh, the wood-saw with which Wood would saw wood! But one day, Wood's wood-saw would saw no wood, and thus the wood Wood sawed was not the wood Wood would saw if Wood's wood-saw would saw wood. Now Wood would saw wood with a wood-saw that would saw wood, so Esau sought a saw that would saw wood. One day, Esau saw a saw saw wood as no other wood-saw Wood saw would saw wood. In fact, of all the wood-saws Wood ever saw saw wood, Wood never saw a wood-saw that would saw wood as the wood-saw Wood saw saw wood would saw wood. And I never saw a wood-saw that would saw as the wood-saw Wood saw would saw until I saw Esau saw wood with the wood-saw Wood saw saw wood.

However, when you add **stress**, **rhythm**, and **intonation** to the story, it suddenly comes alive and makes sense.

Instructions:
1. Listen to your instructor read through "The Story of Esau Wood." Use a slash mark to separate the words that belong in a phrase. The first sentence has been done for you.

2. Put a stress mark over the word in each phrase that carries the stress for that phrase.

3. Draw an arrow to indicate all the places where there is falling intonation or rising intonation.

1. Esau **Wóod /** sawed **wóod**.

2. Esau Wood would saw wood.

3. All the wood Esau Wood saw, Esau Wood would saw.

4. In other words, all the wood Esau saw to saw, Esau sought to saw.

5. Oh, the wood Wood would saw!

6. And oh, the wood-saw with which Wood would saw wood!

A very sharp and powerful saw!

7. But one day, Wood's wood-saw would saw no wood, and thus the wood Wood sawed was not the wood Wood would saw if Wood's wood-saw would saw wood.

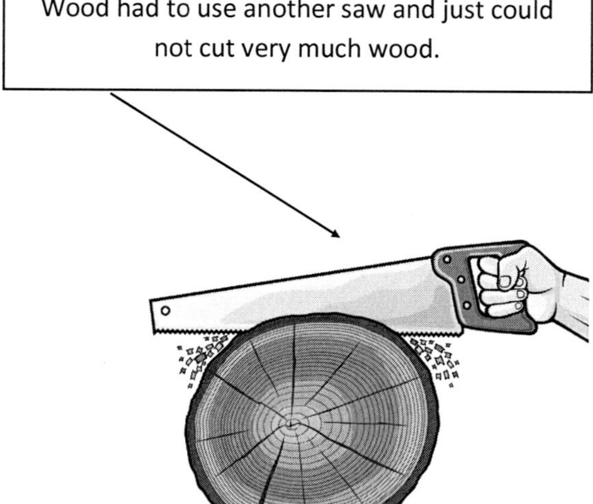

8. Now Wood would saw wood with a wood-saw that would saw wood, so Esau sought a saw that would saw wood.

9. One day, Esau saw a saw saw wood as no other wood-saw Wood saw would saw wood.

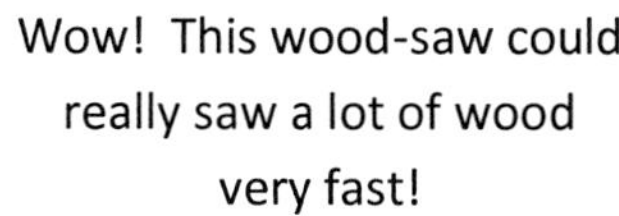

10. In fact, of all the wood-saws Wood ever saw saw wood, Wood never saw a wood-saw that would saw wood as the wood-saw Wood saw saw wood would saw wood.

11. And I never saw a wood-saw that would saw as the wood-saw Wood saw would saw until I saw Esau saw

wood with the wood-saw Wood saw saw wood.

12. Now, Wood saws wood with the wood-saw Wood saw saw wood.

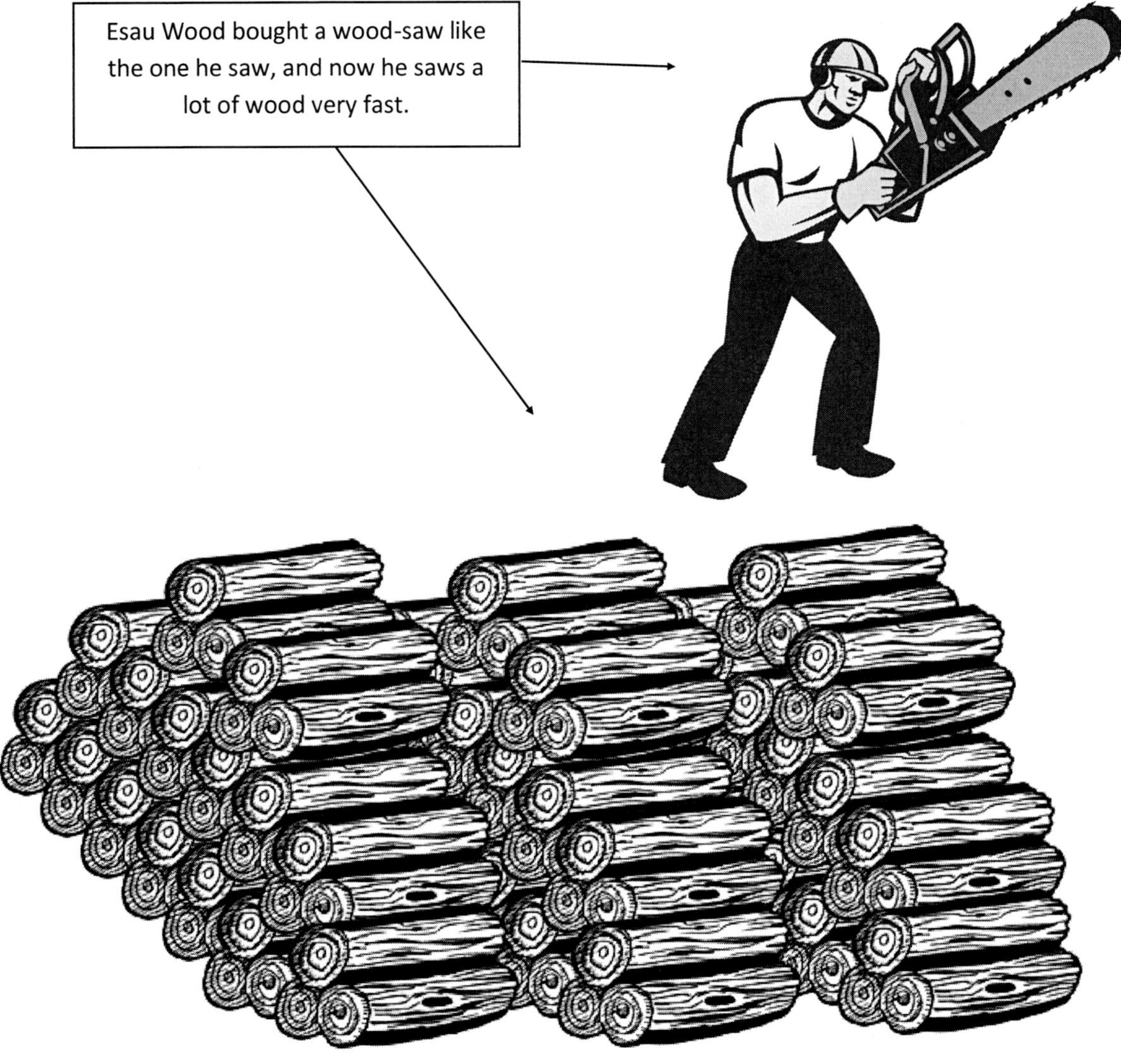

"THE STORY OF ESAU WOOD" - ANSWER KEY

1. Esau **Wóod** / sawed **wóod**.

2. Esau **Wóod** / **wóuld** saw wood.

3. All the **wóod** / Esau Wood **sáw**, / Esau **Wóod** / **wóuld** saw.

4. In **óther** words, / all the **wóod** / Esau **sáw** to saw, /

   Esau **sóught** to saw.

5. Oh, the **wóod** / **Wóod** would **sáw**!

6. And **óh**, / the **wóod**-saw / with which **Wóod** / **wóuld** saw **wóod**!

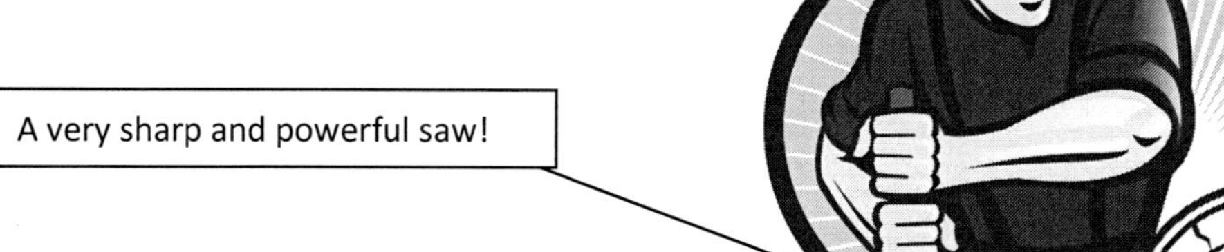

A very sharp and powerful saw!

7. But **óne** day, / Wood's **wóod**-saw/ would **sáw** no **wóod**, / and thus the **wóod** / Wood **sáwed** /

was **nót** the wood **/** Wood **wóuld** saw **/** if Wood's **wóod**-saw **/** **wóuld** saw **wóod**.

8. Now **Wóod /**would **sáw** wood /with a **wóod**-saw **/** that **wóuld** saw wood,

so Esau **sóught** a saw **/** that **wóuld** saw **wóod**.

9. **Óne** day, **/** Esau **sáw** a saw **/** **sáw wóod /** as **nó** other **wóod**-saw **/** Wood **sáw / wóuld** saw **wóod**.

10. In **fáct**, **/** of **áll** the **wóod**-saws **/** Wood **éver** saw / **sáw** wood;

Wood **néver** saw a **wóod**-saw **/** that would saw **wóod /** as the **wóod**-saw**/**

Wood **sáw** saw wood **/** would **sáw** wood.

11. And I **néver** saw a **wóod**-saw **/** that would **sáw /** as the **wóod**-saw **/** Wood **sáw** would saw **/**

   úntil I saw **Esáu /** saw **wóod /** with the **wóod**-saw **/** Wood **sáw** saw wood.

12. Now, **/ Wóod** saws **wóod /**with the **wóod**-saw **/** Wood **sáw /** saw wood.

DON'T GET THESE MIXED UP: *USE/USED, USE TO/USED TO, BE USED TO*

Not only do these expressions have different meanings,
each has its own pronunciation, stress, and rhythm.

1. *Use/Used*

   - verb

   - stress is on the <u>verb</u>: She USES/USED the subway.

   - *use* /yuz/ *used* /yuzd/

        a) What resources do you *use* for your classes?

        b) She *uses* a hair dryer every morning.

        c) I am *using* a computer to write this sentence.

        d) I *used* the telephone five minutes ago.

        e) I *used* a coat this morning because it was cold.

2. *Use to/Used to* + Verb

   - use as a VERB to mean "done before, but not anymore"; most always used in "past tense" form

   - stress is on <u>use/used</u>: He USED to live in New York. Did he USE to live in New York?

   - *used to* /yustu/—you do not pronounce the "d"; *use to* /yustu/

        a) I *used to* ride a bicycle when I was a child, but I don't ride one anymore.

        b) I *used to* get up at 6:00 in the morning, but now I get up at 7:00.

        c) Use the base form with negatives and questions:
            What did you *use to* do when you lived in China? Did you *use to* drive a car in China?
            No, I didn't *use to* drive a car there.

3. *BE Used to* + Noun/Gerund

   - use as an ADJECTIVE to mean "to be familiar with/accustomed to/comfortable with"

   - stress is on <u>used</u>: I am USED to eating breakfast at 7:00 AM.

   - am/is/are/was/were + *used to* /yustu/—you do not pronounce the "d"

        a) I *am used to* the snow; it doesn't bother me.

        b) He *is used to* getting up at 5:00 every morning, so he doesn't mind.

        c) The students *aren't used to* the new teacher, but I'm sure they will like him.

        d) Noriko *is used to* the road near her house, and she knows how to avoid every bump.

        e) What *are* you *used to*?

PART V:

IDIOMATIC EXPRESSIONS

IDIOMATIC EXPRESSIONS

(Meanings and origins are not cited unless the information is unique or not commonly known.)

① pp. 141-170: animal-based expressions

Because Anna asked for a transfer,

her boss was <u>loaded for bear</u> in the staff
①
meeting, so she decided to <u>hold her tongue;</u>
②
otherwise, she could <u>get the axe</u>.
③

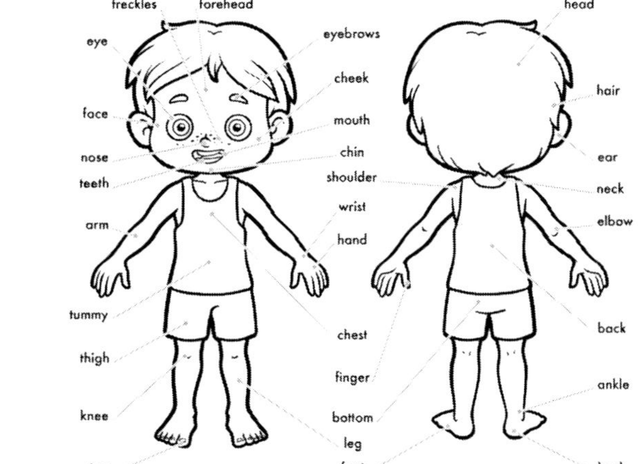

② pp. 171-174: body-based expressions

③ pp. 175-178: work-based expressions and jargon

ANIMALS ARE HIDING IN MY ENGLISH!: ANIMAL-BASED EXPRESSIONS

(meanings and sample sentences begin on page 145)

ANIMALS	SIMILIES ADJECTIVES NOUNS	VERBS	IDIOMS
ant	1. antsy	2. have ants in [your] pants	
bat	3. as blind as a bat 4. like a bat out of Hell 5. batty	6. have bats in [your] belfry	
bear	7. hungry as a bear 8. like a mother bear 9. a bear hug		10. He's loaded for bear.
beaver	11. as busy as a beaver 12. a busy beaver 13. an eager beaver	14. beaver away	
bed bug			15. Sleep tight; don't let the bedbugs bite.
bee	16. as busy as a bee 17. like a bee to honey	18. make a bee line for. . .	19. Mind your own beeswax.
bird	20. as free as a bird 21. eat like a bird 22. sing like a bird 23. for the birds 24. a bird's eye view 25. an early bird		26. A little bird told me. 27. Birds of a feather flock together. 28. A bird in the hand is worth two in the bush. 29. The early bird catches the worm.
bug	30. snug as a bug in a rug	31. put a bug in someone's ear	
bull	32. like a bull in a china shop 33. bull-headed	34. take the bull by the horns 35. hit the bull's eye	
butterfly	36. a social butterfly	37. have butterflies in [my] stomach	
camel		38. strain at gnats but swallow a camel	39. It's easier to get a camel through the eye of a needle than + V. . .

ANIMALS	SIMILIES ADJECTIVES NOUNS	VERBS	IDIOMS
			40. It's the straw that broke the camel's back.
canary	41. like a canary in a coal mine		
cat	42. like herding cats 43. like a cat on a hot tin roof 44. like the cat that swallowed the canary 45. catty 46. a cat nap 47. a copy cat		48. The cat's in the bag. 49. Look at what the cat dragged in! 50. Don't let the cat out of the bag! 51. The cat's got [his] tongue. 52. Cat got [your] tongue? 53. It's raining cats and dogs! 54. Curiosity killed the cat.
chicken	55. like a chicken with its head cut off 56. chicken-hearted	57. chicken out	
clam	58. as happy as a clam	59. clam up	
cow		60. talk till the cows come home	
deer	61. like a deer in the headlights		
dog	62. as sick as a dog 63. dog tired 64. a top dog	65. go to the dogs	66. It's a dog's life. 67. It's a dog-eat-dog world. 68. You can't teach an old dog new tricks. 69. It's raining cats and dogs. 70. Let sleeping dogs lie.
duck	71. like water off a duck's back 72. waddle like a duck 73. a sitting duck	74. Duck!	
eagle	75. soar like an eagle		
eel	76. as slippery as an eel		
elephant	77. the elephant in the room		
fish	78. like a fish out of water 79. swim like a fish 80. fishy 81. a big fish in a small pond	82. have other/bigger fish to fry 83. fish for something 84. fish for a compliment 85. go on a fishing expedition	86. Fish or cut bait. 87. There's plenty of other fish in the sea.

ANIMALS	SIMILIES ADJECTIVES NOUNS	VERBS	IDIOMS
fly	88. dropping like flies		89. I'd like to be a fly on the wall.
fox	90. as sly as a fox		91. You sly fox!
frog			92. I have a frog in my throat.
goat		93. get someone's goat	
goose	94. as silly as a goose 95. goose bumps	96. go on a wild goose chase	97. You silly goose!
hen	98. as scarce as hen's teeth		
hog	99. eat like a hog 100. a road hog	101. live high on the hog 102. go hog-wild	
hornet	103. as mad as a hornet	104. stir up a hornet's nest	
horse	105. as healthy as a horse 106. eat like a horse 107. a charley horse 108. a horse of a different color 109. horse sense	110. get back up on the horse 111. see a man about a horse	112. Don't look a gift horse in the mouth! 113. Don't swap horses in the middle of the stream! 114. I got it straight from the horse's mouth. 115. Hold [your] horses! 116. You can lead a horse to water, but you can't make him drink. 117. Don't put the cart before the horse. 118. Quit horsing around! 119. Get off your high horse!
lamb	120. as gentle/innocent/meek as a lamb 121. like a lamb to the slaughter		122. I'll do it in two shakes of a lamb's tail.
leopard			123. A leopard can't change its spots.
lion	124. as brave as a lion	125. get the lion's share of sth.	
lobster	126. as red as a lobster		
loon	127. as crazy as a loon		
mouse	128. as silent/quiet as a mouse 129. mousey	130. play cat and mouse with. . .	

ANIMALS	SIMILIES ADJECTIVES NOUNS	VERBS	IDIOMS
monkey	131. monkey business	132. make a monkey out of sb.	133. Monkey see, monkey do.
mule	134. as stubborn as a mule		
owl	135. as wise as an owl		
ox	136. as strong as an ox	137. have an ox in the ditch	
oyster			138. The world's [your] oyster.
peacock	139. as proud as a peacock		
pig	140. piggy-back	141. pig out	142. When pigs fly!
pony	143. a one-trick pony		144. It's a one-pony show/circus.
rabbit	145. as fast as a rabbit 146. a rabbit trail	147. pull a rabbit out of a hat 148. go down a rabbit hole	
rat	149. like rats deserting a sinking ship 150. a rat race	151. smell a rat 152. rat on/out someone	
rooster		153. strut around like a banty rooster	
sardine	154. packed in like sardines		
sheep	155. like a sheep among wolves 156. follow like sheep 157. sheepish	158. separate the sheep from the goats 159. count sheep	160. He's the black sheep of the family.
snake	161. a snake in the grass		162. If it were a snake, it would bite you.
swan	163. as graceful as a swan		
tiger	164. like having a tiger by the tail	165. put a tiger in [your] tank	166. A tiger cannot change its stripes.
turtle	167. as slow as a turtle		
weasel		168. weasel out of/into something	169. You weasel!
whale	170. a whale of a------		
wolf	171. a lone wolf 172. a wolf in sheep's clothing	173. throw someone to the wolves 174. cry wolf (cry, "Wolf!")	
worm	175. a book worm	176. worm [your] way out of/into sth.	

SIMILIE/EXPRESSION/IDIOM	MEANING	SAMPLE SENTENCE
1. **ant**sy	• nervous with anticipation • scurrying around like ants	She was *antsy* before the performance.
2. have **ants** in your pants	• cannot be/sit still • nervous	He had *ants in his pants* before speaking in front of the group.
3. as blind as a **bat**	ORIGIN: bats have very bad eyesight during daylight hours • unable to see well • unable to notice the obvious	Because she's *as blind as a bat*, she thought the raccoon was her cat.
4. like a **bat** out of Hell	ORIGIN: bats have long been associated with witches, the occult, evil, and dark spaces, so, they might hurriedly avoid the light of the "fires of Hell" • leave a place recklessly fast	When he saw his ex-girlfriend at the party, he got out of there *like a bat out of Hell*.
5. **bat**ty	• not making any sense • very confused/acting "crazy"	The old woman was clearly *batty* because she thought I was an alien with two heads.
6. have **bats** in your belfry	ORIGIN: bats fly around erratically In a belfry (a bell tower) • eccentric/unable to think clearly • erratic	The children in the neighborhood thought the man in the old house surely *had bats in his belfry* because he danced in a clown suit in his yard.
7. hungry as a **bear**	ORIGIN: bears hibernate all winter and when they emerge, they are starving • very hungry	He was *as hungry as a bear* after the long hike.
8. like a mother **bear**	• very protective of [your] children	My friend is quick to protect her children against any slight danger; she's *like a mother bear*.
9. a **bear** hug	• a big warm, cozy hug	My mom gave me a big *bear hug* after I failed my test.
10. He's loaded for **bear**.	ORIGIN: to hunt a bear, you must have the right ammunition and a loaded gun, and be ready • ready for an argument or a fight	After the employee lost his job to a younger man, he was *loaded for bear*.

SIMILIE/EXPRESSION/IDIOM	MEANING	SAMPLE SENTENCE
11. as busy as a **beaver**	ORIGIN: beavers are very industrious • working very hard	My friend has been *as busy as a beaver* preparing for her grandchildren's visit.
12. a busy **beaver**	• someone who is very busy	My young son is *a busy beaver* building his tree house.
13. an eager **beaver**	• someone who is very excited about something	He was an *eager beaver* waiting to see his new baby brother.
14. **beaver** away	• work very tirelessly on sth.	He *beavered away* for 10 years to become a skilled carpenter.
15. Sleep tight; don't let the **bedbugs** bite.	• a wish that someone has a good night's sleep	The mother told her children, *"Sleep tight and don't let the bedbugs bite."*
16. as busy as a **bee**	ORIGIN: bees are very industrious/productive • being very busy and productive	The students were *as busy as bees* planning for their class party.
17. like a **bee** to honey	ORIGIN: bees naturally return to their hive where there is honey • very attracted to something	He went after that job offer *like a bee to honey.*
18. make a **bee** line for	ORIGIN: bees fly the most direct route to bring nectar and pollen back to their hives • take the shortest distance between two points	After watching a long baseball game, he *made a bee line for* the hot dog stand.
19. Mind your own **bee**swax.	ORIGIN: possibly associated with the old tradition of women gathering together to make candles out of bee's wax • pay attention to your own business/family	The old woman always wanted to know what was going on with her friends, but hey told her to *mind her own beeswax.*
20. as free as a **bird**	• enjoy going somewhere without any boundaries or restrictions	After his divorce, he felt *as free as a bird.*
21. eat like a **bird**	• eat very little	My friend is so thin; she *eats like a bird.*
22. sing like a **bird**	• sing easily and happily	My young daughter *sings like a bird.*

SIMILIE/EXPRESSION/IDIOM	MEANING	SAMPLE SENTENCE
23. for the **birds**	ORIGIN: birds eat bird seed, which is cheap • undesirable/poor quality/cheap • not worth cost /effort/time	I thought the topic for the women's meeting was *for the birds.*
24. a **bird's** eye view	• a view of something from above	I had *a bird's eye view* of Paris from the Eiffel Tower.
25. an early **bird**	• someone who gets up early in the morning	My father is *an early bird* because he always gets up at 4:00AM.
26. A little **bird** told [me].	• said about [sb.] who heard a secret from sb.	*A little bird told me* that you are getting married.
27. **Birds** of a feather flock together.	ORIGIN: birds fly together with their own kind • said about people who look, act, or think alike	When my father saw me with my friends, he said, *"Birds of a feather flock together."*
28. A **bird** in the hand is worth two in the bush.	• advice about valuing what you already have rather than wishing for something better that might not happen or you might not receive	*A bird in the hand is worth two in the bush,* so In this economy, the job I currently have is better than whatever else is out there.
29. The early **bird** catches the worm.	• advice for someone to take advantage of opportunities when they first appear	She was the first one in line for the job interviews because she believes that *the early bird catches the worm.*
30. snug as a **bug** in a rug	• very comfortable and cozy	When it's cold outside, I wrap up in a nice blanket and stay *as snug as a bug in a rug.*
31. put a **bug** in someone's ear	• to give someone early or previously unknown information about sth.	I knew about the job opportunity before Thomas because my friend had *put a bug in my ear.*
32. like a **bull** in a china-shop	ORIGIN: a china shop sells delicate and expensive dishware (china), which is easily broken • very clumsy • likely to break something or bump into things	When my husband went shopping with me, he was *like a bull in a china shop.*
33. **bull**-headed	ORIGIN: bulls are persistent, steady, and strong-willed; they prefer to be left alone and not be bothered; this is seen as stubbornness • stubborn, obstinate, persistent	My boss is *bull-headed* and will not listen to any new ideas for the company.

SIMILIE/EXPRESSION/IDIOM	MEANING	SAMPLE SENTENCE
34. take the **bull** by the horns	<ul><li>aggressively pursue a risky project or opportunity</li><li>decisive/confident</li></ul>	He decided to *take the bull by the horns* and buy the new company.
35. hit the **bull**seye	ORIGIN: the center of an archery target is called the "bull's eye"<ul><li>say or do something exactly right/meet a goal</li><li>hit the center of a target</li></ul>	He *hit the bull's eye* by finally figuring out how to connect all the new equipment.
36. a social **butterfly**	<ul><li>sb. who is overly friendly with many people</li><li>sb. who seek lots of social activities</li><li>sb. trying to meet a lot of people at a party</li></ul>	Jennifer has been to lots of parties this month; she's a real *social butterfly.*
37. have **butterflies** in [my] stomach	<ul><li>be really nervous about something</li></ul>	Before she got up to sing, she *had butterflies in her stomach.*
38. strain at gnats but swallow a **camel**	<ul><li>worry about/focus on annoying details but ignore bigger, more important things</li></ul>	He was *straining at gnats but swallowing a camel* when he fussed about the color of his dying father's hospital room.
39. It's easier for a **camel** to go through the eye of a needle than + V. . .	ORIGIN: the opening of a sewing needle is very small and narrow, and a camel is quite tall; an unproven theory claims there was a small, narrow gate in Jerusalem that would allow people to pass through when the main gate was closed; a camel would have to stoop very low and unload its baggage to go through the opening<ul><li>impossible to accomplish a particular task</li><li>humble oneself to do sth.</li></ul>https://en.wikipedia.org/wiki/Eye_of_a_needle	It is *easier for a camel to go through the eye of a needle* than to get my son to clean his room.
40. It was the straw that broke the **camel's** back.	ORIGIN: a camel can typically carry very heavy loads, but adding just one more item could exceed its physical limit<ul><li>too many small tasks can add up to an unmanageable burden</li><li>the final "sth." that is just too much for sb. to deal with</li></ul>	James was typically late for work, and this last time was *the straw that broke the camel's back;* he was fired.

SIMILIE/EXPRESSION/IDIOM	MEANING	SAMPLE SENTENCE
41. like a **canary** in a coal mine	ORIGIN: canaries are sent into a coal mine before the workers enter in order to detect the presence of gas; if present, the gas kills the canary before killing the miners. • sth./sb. used to detect or determine a possible risk to a person or project	John was *like a canary in a coal mine* when he agreed to test a new drug for his specific illness.
42. like herding **cats**	ORIGIN: cats can be stubborn and are not easily led; they have a mind of their own • trying to lead a group of independent people is not easy	Trying to get all the members of the tour group back on the bus was *like herding cats*.
43. like a **cat** on a hot tin roof	• very nervous or agitated • wanting to get away from something in a hurry	The big social event she organized was a disaster because she was *like a cat on a hot tin roof*.
44. like the **cat** that swallowed the canary	ORIGIN: cats are often shown in photos or cartoons looking hopefully at a bird in a cage, often a canary; if indeed the cat actually is able to get the bird, he will be very pleased and may even proudly hold the bird in its mouth while the angry/shocked owner looks on • appearing self-satisfied or smug especially while trying to hide something mischievous • reaction to a surprising accomplishment	The little boy, covered with chocolate, looked *like the cat that swallowed the canary*.
45. **catt**y	ORIGIN: cats can be sly, spiteful, and mean • acting spiteful/nasty; ill-tempered • malicious/insulting/offensive	The girls in the school cafeteria made *catty* remarks about the new foreign student at the table.
46. a **cat** nap	ORIGIN: cats are well known for sleeping for long periods as well as for a few minutes at a time • a short nap	Jonathan must work long hours, so he frequently takes *cat naps* throughout the day; they help him stay alert.
47. a copy **cat**	• a person who imitates sb. else	Samantha gave the same speech for her class that Jennifer had given a year ago; Jennifer called her *a copy cat*.

SIMILIE/EXPRESSION/IDIOM	MEANING	SAMPLE SENTENCE
48. a **cat** burglar	• thief who silently breaks into buildings by climbing on roofs or entering through upstairs windows • thief who has great agility, like a cat	A *cat burglar* quietly entered the house through a second-story window and stole all the jewelry while the party was going on.
49. Look at what the **cat** dragged in!	ORIGIN: cats often proudly bring their dead prey (birds, mice, snakes) into the house to show their owner • a statement of surprise at sth. or sb. that is nasty, ugly, smelly, rumpled, dirty, offensive	After Mike had hiked all day in the mountain s and in the rain, his mother said, *"Look at what the cat dragged in!"* when he returned home
50. Don't let the **cat** out of the bag!	• warning not to reveal sth. that is a secret or a surprise	The teacher told the class, *"Don't let the cat out of the bag!"* after she announced that they would give a surprise performance for the whole school.
51. The **cat's** got [his] tongue? 52. Cat got [your] tongue?	• said of sb. who seems unable to say anything • Don't you have anything to say?	When she was offered the unexpected check for $1000.00, it was as if the *cat got her tongue*; she was speechless.
53. It's raining **cats** and dogs!	ORIGIN: it is said that cats and dogs would often sleep in the grass or thatched roofs of houses; when it would rain heavily, the animals would be washed out of the roof area and into the living area • said when it's raining heavily	The skies opened up, and we got three inches of rain an hour; it was definitely *raining cats and dogs*.
54. Curiosity killed the cat.	• a warning to avoid unnecessary experimentation or investigation • there are consequences to being too curious	When I wanted to go inside an abandoned house, my friend reminded me that *curiosity killed the cat* and that I should be careful.
55. like a **chicken** with its head cut off	ORIGIN: occasionally, when a chicken's head is chopped off, its body will actually run around in an uncontrollable manner before it dies. • to do sth. in a crazy or frenzied manner/ appear to be without plan or purpose	When she heard the news that her husband was finally coming home from his military assignment, she *ran around like a chicken with its head cut off* trying to get everything ready in a short time.

SIMILIE/EXPRESSION/IDIOM	MEANING	SAMPLE SENTENCE
56. **chicken**-hearted	• cowardly/afraid	Those boys called my 10-year old brother *chicken -hearted* because he wouldn't try to drive my father's car.
57. **chicken** out	• to change one's mind because of fear or lack of confidence	She climbed the ladder to the very high diving board and then *chickened out;* she wouldn't dive into the water.
58. as happy as a **clam**	ORIGINALLY "as happy as a clam at high tide" meaning a clam didn't have to worry about predators if it was in deep water • happy, content, secure	The children were *as happy as clams* when the teacher let them watch cartoons.
59. **clam** up	• be quite/quit talking • reveal nothing	The criminal *clammed up* when the police started asking him questions.
60. [talk] till the **cows** come home	ORIGIN: when cows are let out into the pasture, it's a long time before they come back to the barn for milking • take an unnecessarily long time to do sth.	When they get together once a year, my aunt and her friends can talk *till the cows came home.*
61. like a **deer** in the headlights	ORIGIN: when a car's headlights shine on a deer in the dark, the deer has a frozen look on its face, and it's eyes are very wide • to show fear or shock on one's face	She looked *like a deer in the headlights* when the thief pointed a gun at her and demanded money.
62. as sick as a **dog**	ORIGIN: dogs frequently vomit ("get sick") if they eat something disagreeable to them • to vomit a lot	When she ate that contaminated lettuce, she *got sick as a dog.*
63. **dog** tired	ORIGIN: Alfred the Great used to have his sons try to catch all his dogs; whichever son brought back the most dogs would be able to sit with his father for dinner; however, they were tired from chasing dogs all day • very tired; exhausted https://www.theidioms.com/dog-tired/	When my mother works a 12-hour shift as a nurse, she comes home *dog tired.*

SIMILIE/EXPRESSION/IDIOM	MEANING	SAMPLE SENTENCE
64. a/the top **dog**	ORIGIN: probably from dog fights in which the more superior and stronger dog was on top of the weaker, more submissive dog. • opposite of "under dog" • stronger/superior/the boss	The employee that showed me around the factory was considered to be the *top dog* by the other employees.
65. go to the **dogs**	ORIGIN: in ancient China, dogs were not permitted within the walls of cities and roamed around outside living on rubbish; criminals and other offenders would be thrown outside the walled cities and forced to live among the dogs, their lives now being ruined. • to be in slow decline • to be worse off than before https://superbeefy.com/how-did-the-expression-gone-to-the-dogs-originate-and-what-does-the-phrase-mean/	The shopping center on the southside of the city *is going to the dogs,* and very few people shop there any more.
66. It's a **dog's** life.	• a comment made about someone who's well-taken care of and has little to worry about • a leisurely life	A relaxing weekend at a spa can feel like a *dog's life* for busy moms.
67. It's a **dog**-eat-**dog** world.	ORIGIN: a contradiction to a Roman proverb that dogs do not eat other dogs. So, to do so would be unnaturally ruthless and competitive. • a very competitive environment in which people do whatever they need to do in order to get ahead in business or politics	The recent campaign ads for the upcoming election resembled a *dog-eat-dog world.*
68. You can't teach an old **dog** new tricks.	ORIGIN: important to teach a sheep dog while it's a puppy to respond to commands; otherwise it won't learn well when older; even though many people do learn new ways of doing things when they're old, this idiom implies the opposite. • a comment made about someone fixed in their particular way of doing things • said of sb. unwilling to change	My grandfather will never use a cell phone or a computer. I guess you *can't teach an old dog new tricks.*
69. It's raining cats and **dogs.**	See #53	

SIMILIE/EXPRESSION/IDIOM	MEANING	SAMPLE SENTENCE
70. Let sleeping **dogs** lie.	ORIGIN: it's not a good idea to suddenly wake up a dog that is sleeping because it can become defensive ● ignore discussing a negative or difficult issue especially when everything else seems fine	At the family reunion this year, Emma asked her grandmother to *let sleeping dogs lie* and not argue with other family members about something that happened years ago.
71. like water off a **duck's** back	ORIGIN: a duck's wing feathers are very oily, so water cannot get through to the inner feathers or the duck's body, and it won't sink ● unaffected or influenced by negative comments or situations	Pat and Ed had studied for the test many hours but failed; they ignored their low results like *water rolling off a duck's back.*
72. waddle like a **duck**	ORIGIN: ducks have a characteristic way of walking due to their webbed feet; this causes the rear part of their body to sway back and forth; similarly, people whose feet are out-turned also tend to walk this way ● walk like a duck ● sway from side to side while walking	Sadly, the children were laughing at that overweight man because he seemed to be *waddling like a duck.*
73. a sitting **duck**	ORIGIN: when hunters are looking for ducks to shoot, a sitting duck is an easy and vulnerable target ● unavoidable target ● vulnerable, unprotected	When someone speaks out against behavior that is unjust or immoral, that person often becomes a *sitting duck* for criticism.
74. **Duck!**	ORIGIN: the verb "duck" came from Old English and means "dive" or "get low"; therefore, because they could dive under the water, certain birds were called "ducks"; the word "duck" is both a verb and a noun ● bend, stoop, or get low ● a warning to get low	The door openings in ancient homes are too low for my husband to comfortably walk through, so our guide yells, "Duck!"
75. soar like an **eagle**	ORIGIN: because eagles seek out "waves" of air to float on, they don't need to use their wings,	Because he knew he had the support of his family, Benjamin *soared like an eagle* through all

SIMILIE/EXPRESSION/IDIOM	MEANING	SAMPLE SENTENCE
	and they glide effortlessly through the sky • unaffected by chaos or turmoil • easily move through trouble of difficulties, often to success	the challenges and difficulties of college; he graduated with honors.
76. as slippery as an **eel**	ORIGIN: eels are long, slimy bony fish; they are predators • difficult to hold or capture • unable to trust, devious, scheming	Finally, the police got information that would help them arrest a jewelry thief; however, he was *as slippery as an eel* and escaped.
77. the **elephant** in the room	ORIGIN: it's very difficult to ignore an elephant • the situation or issue that no one wants to discuss, mention, or talk about	Because his daughter died last year, not talking about her absence at the family reunion was like ignoring *the elephant in the room.*
78. like a **fish** out of water	ORIGIN: when a fish is taken out of water, it flounders and flaps around until its gills dry and it essentially suffocates • in unfamiliar surroundings • awkward; uncertain about what to do	When he followed his doctor's orders and went to the gym to exercise for the first time, he felt *like a fish out of water*; he had never been to a gym before.
79. swim like a **fish**	ORIGIN: fish swim very efficiently and easily • swim very well • do sth. effortlessly and efficiently; easily	Because the company had to fill the supervisor's position immediately, they asked their best factory worker to take the position; he jumped into the new situation and *swam like a fish.*
80. **fish**y	ORIGIN: if meat has a "fishy" taste, people know the meat is spoiled; something's wrong with it • suspicious/out of the ordinary • doubtful	My son gave me a *fishy* explanation about why he no longer had the money I gave him.
81. a big **fish** in a small pond	ORIGIN: a big fish in a small pond is easily prominent and noticeable, and it tends to dominate the smaller fish • an important and influential person in a limited or somewhat unimportant arena • sb. who is over-qualified for sth.	Even with all his education and training, he still preferred to work in the small rural community, so he was *a big fish in a small pond.*

SIMILIE/EXPRESSION/IDIOM	MEANING	SAMPLE SENTENCE
82. have bigger **fish** to fry	ORIGIN: you don't bother cooking small fish if you have larger ones with more meat on them • spend time and energy on more important or beneficial activities • to not be distracted by less important issues	Police sometimes choose to overlook smaller crimes because *they have bigger fish to fry.*
83. **fish** for something	• making a comment or doing sth. deliberately to make sb. "bite" and give you what you want	My boss finally gave in when he realized I was *fishing* for a promotion.
84. **fish** for a compliment	• say or do sth. in order for someone to give you a compliment	After the wife *fished for a compliment f*rom her husband, he finally told her she looked nice.
85. go on a **fish**ing expedition	• look for sth. specific • See #83	Trying to find the paperwork for the original purchase of my house was like *going on a fishing expedition.*
86. **Fish** or cut bait.	• do the work or help, but don't just stand there.	When I was just standing around watching my dad, he said, *"Fish or cut bait."* He didn't want me to be lazy.
87. There's plenty of other **fish** in the sea.	• this person/job/opportunity is surely not the only choice.	After my boyfriend broke up with me, my friend said, *"There's plenty of other fish in the sea."*
88. dropping like **flies**	ORIGIN: flies appear in large numbers but can die quickly • many people collapsing/giving up/quitting/ not doing well	The contestants were *dropping like flies* at the Spelling Competition until a 10-year old won.
89. I'd like to be a **fly** on the wall.	• be able to be inconspicuous and listen to or watch sb./sth.	When my brother explains to our father why he came home so late, *I'd like to be a fly on the wall.*
90. as sly as a **fox**	ORIGIN: a fox is known for being tricky and cunning • be clever/cunning/smart	The jewelry thief was *as sly as a fox* and never got caught.
91. You sly **fox**!	• said of sb. who successfully deceived or tricked sb. else	When the boyfriend finally proposed to his reluctant girlfriend, his good friend said,

SIMILIE/EXPRESSION/IDIOM	MEANING	SAMPLE SENTENCE
	• See #90	*"You sly fox!"*
92. I have a **frog** in my throat.	• making a raspy/hoarse sound —rather like a frog—due to a sore throat	I can't give my speech today because *I have a frog in my throat,* and no one will understand me.
93. get someone's **goat**	ORIGIN: thought to refer to practice of putting goats in stables with race horses to calm the horses before a race; if the goat got stolen, the horse would have a restless night and likely lose the race the next day • cause sb. to be annoyed/irritated/disturbed http://www.dictionary.com/browse/get-someone-s-goat	My boss really *got my goat* when she told me I wouldn't be able to earn overtime pay.
94. as silly as a **goose**	ORIGIN: geese can make a lot of noise and walk around in circles, looking silly • foolish/ignorant/stupid	I thought my grandmother was *as silly as a goose* because she walked around mumbling to herself.
95. **goose** bumps	ORIGIN: when a goose's feathers are plucked, they leave bumps on the skin • bumpy/raised skin caused by fear or shock (pilomotor reflex) • skin resembling a plucked goose https://en.wikipedia.org/wiki/Goose_bumps	Watching a scary movie always gives me *goose bumps.*
96. go on a wild **goose** chase	ORIGIN: a "wild goose chase" was once a horse race in which horses followed a lead horse like geese in formation; this led to a wild and somewhat disorganized race • a pointless, unsuccessful pursuit • like chasing wild geese	Looking for my dog who was chasing a rabbit was like *going on a wild goose chase.*
97. You silly **goose**!	• See #94 • a term of endearment	*"You silly goose!* the mom said when she found her two-year old son covered with peanut butter and jelly after he tried to make a sandwich.
98. as scarce as **hen's** teeth	ORIGIN: hens do not have teeth • very scarce/rare/non-existent	A's on my son's grade report are *as scarce as hen's teeth.*
99. eat like a **hog**	ORIGIN: hogs eat a lot and are sloppy eaters • eat a lot of food in a sloppy manner • See #141	My teenage sons always *ate like hogs.*

SIMILIE/EXPRESSION/IDIOM	MEANING	SAMPLE SENTENCE
100. a road **hog**	• a driver who takes too much space on the road while driving and makes it unsafe for other drivers	The man in front of me on the highway was *a road hog*; he kept swerving from one lane to another.
101. live high on the **hog**	ORIGIN: the meat above the belly of a hog is the most tender, costly, and delicious to eat • only the best • to have the good things of life	Now that she has a better-paying job, she's *living high on the hog*.
102. go **hog**-wild	• run around like wild hogs • excessive, unrestrained excitement	The day after school was out, all the children ran *hog-wild* around the neighborhood
103. as mad as a **hornet**	ORIGIN: when a hornet's nest is disturbed, the hornets fly out angrily and offensively • really mad	My mom was *mad as a hornet* when I forgot to pick up my little brother after school.
104. stir up a **hornet's** nest	• agitate/make sb.angry over sth. no one wants to talk about • See #103	Don't bring up that topic in the meeting because you'll be *stirring up a hornet's nest*.
105. as healthy as a **horse**	ORIGIN: a well-fed horse is seen as symbol of strength and physical ability and becomes a beautiful animal to be admired; horses are herbivores • healthy/strong/capable	Don't worry about his diet because he eats *as healthy as a horse*.
106. eat like a **horse**	• See #105	*Eat like a horse,* and you'll be just fine.
107. a charley **horse**	ORIGIN: possibly because a baseball player named Charley Radbourne, who was nicknamed Old Hoss (for horse), got a leg cramp/muscle spasm during a game in the 1880's; hence the name "charley horse" • a cramp/muscle spasm https://www.phrases.org.uk/meanings/charley-horse.html	We had to stop playing volleyball because I got *a charley horse* in my right leg.
108. a **horse** of a different color	• sb./sth. different from the others else but within the same category	Your sister is really *a horse of a different color* and doesn't seem to fit in your family.

SIMILIE/EXPRESSION/IDIOM	MEANING	SAMPLE SENTENCE
109. **horse** sense	ORIGIN: American west depended upon the good sense of a horse; horses seem to know what they should do, but they can have a mind of their own • common sense • prudence/practical thinking	You can depend on that new guy because he's got a lot of *horse sense*.
110. get back up on the **horse**	ORIGIN: if you remount a horse that you have fallen off of, you show confidence and strength and control to the horse • try a challenging effort again • avoid being defeated by failure	After several attempts at finding a job, the man was encouraged to *get back up on the horse* and try again.
111. see a man about a **horse**	ORIGIN: heard during the Prohibition Era in the US when sb. would use this phrase as a reason to depart for some secret meeting probably about buying or selling illegal alcohol; horses were common in rural areas, so it was not unrealistic for sb. to make a deal about a horse • often said prior to going to the restroom or beginning some private/personal activity • said when you don't want sb. to know where you're going	He politely said, *"I've got to see a man about a horse,"* when he left the restaurant, but I saw him outside with another woman, not his wife.
112. Don't look a gift **horse** in the mouth.	ORIGIN: common practice when buying and selling horses to look at a horse's teeth to determine its age and health • appreciate the value of a gift given to you without questioning or double-checking	Although the boyfriend won the string of pearls at a carnival, and they were not genuine, his girlfriend was determined not to *look a gift horse in the mouth* and proudly wore them.
113. Don't swap **horses** in the middle of the stream!	ORIGIN: although this phrase originated earlier, it was popularized by Abraham Lincoln in 1864 as he reflected on why he was being nominated again for President; actually changing horses in the middle of a stream can be awkward, dangerous, and unsuccessful • make major changes in an activity after it	When the former manager had a heart attack while working on a large sales contract, the CEO did not want to *swap horses in the middle of the stream,* but he had no choice; the transition to a new manager was very difficult for everyone.

SIMILIE/EXPRESSION/IDIOM	MEANING	SAMPLE SENTENCE
	has already begun • a caution about choosing a new leader in the middle of upheaval or uncertain times	
114. I got it straight from the **horse's** mouth.	ORIGIN: the information you need to determine the health of a horse is from it's mouth • See #112 • get your information from the original source • avoid relying on second-hand information	*I got it straight from the horse's mouth that we will have a new CEO next month; our current CEO told me he is retiring.*
115. Hold [your] **horses**!	ORIGIN: can simply refer to holding horses still and calm during a battle or other situation • avoid rushing into anything too quickly • stay calm and still during something uncertain	The children were told to *hold their horses* before they were allowed to get off the bus and play in the park; the teacher had to record every child's name first.
116. You can lead a **horse** to water, but you can't make it drink.	ORIGIN: an old proverb from the 12th century referring to the "stubbornness" of a horse in determining what, how, and when he will do sth. • providing opportunities for sb. doesn't mean he/she will take advantage of them.	I kept showing my brother newspaper ads for the kinds of jobs he wanted, but he never seemed to pursue them; I guess that proves *you can lead a horse to water, but you can't make it drink.*
117. Don't put the cart before the **horse**.	ORIGIN: a cart is always pulled by a horse and follows the horse; this proverb refers to doing sth.in the wrong order • do sth. contrary to the conventional or expected order • hurry to get sth. done, but in the wrong way	Buying a new car before you sell the old one might be like *putting the cart before the horse.*
118. Quit **horsing** around!	ORIGIN: "horse", as a verb, means to play in a "rough" or "coarse" manner; horses enjoy running, frolicking and jumping often with no warning or reason • play in a rough or wild way • misbehave in a silly manner	When the teacher came back to the classroom after being gone for only a few minutes, she had to tell the misbehaving students to *quit horsing around.*

SIMILIE/EXPRESSION/IDIOM	MEANING	SAMPLE SENTENCE
119. Get off [your] high **horse**!	ORIGIN: In medieval England, a person's rank was reflected by the size of the horse he rode. A noble or a person of importance would ride a large and expensive horse, one much taller and bigger than the horses ridden by commoners, so the person was considered superior • Quit acting so superior! • consider [yourself] superior to others https://www.quora.com/What-is-the-origin-of-the-phrase-get-off-your-high-horse	After my sister won a scholarship to a famous university, she started acting superior to me; I told her to *get off her high horse* and start treating me as an equal again.
120. as gentle/innocent/meek as a **lamb**	ORIGIN: a lamb is considered to be soft/gentle/calming/non-aggressive • non-aggressive, calm • kind, helpful	That big, rough football player is really *as gentle as a lamb*, especially with his children.
121. like a **lamb** to the slaughter	ORIGIN: lambs go calmly up a ramp to be slaughtered because they have no idea what's coming; they're innocent • like walking calmly and innocently into a situation without knowing what's coming • innocent	The student walked into the headmaster's office *like a lamb to the slaughter.*
122. I'll do it in two shakes of a **lamb's** tail.	ORIGIN: "shake" was recognized in the 1920's as a unit of time smaller than a minute and equal to how quickly a lamb could move its tail once • in a very quick amount of time • quicker than a minute https://www.quora.com/What-is-the-origin-of-the-expression-two-shakes-of-a-lambs-tail	When my mom asked me to clean up the kitchen, I said, *"I'll do it in two shakes of a lamb's tail."*
123. A **leopard** can't change its spots.	ORIGIN: a leopard cannot change the spots on its skin (from Jerimiah 13:23 in the Old Testament) • unable to change one's basic nature or character/behavior • negatively said about sb. trying to change	No matter how often my boyfriend talked to his pet snake or treated it kindly, it bit him one day, so I guess *a leopard can't change it's spots* even if it's a snake.

SIMILIE/EXPRESSION/IDIOM	MEANING	SAMPLE SENTENCE
124. as brave as a **lion**	ORIGIN: most cultures consider a lion to be a symbol of strength and bravery; courageous in the face of danger • brave, courageous, bold • not timid/shy	When those bigger and older guys at school started bullying me, my little brother began to fight them; he was *as brave as a lion.*
125. get the **lion's** share of sth.	ORIGIN: from one of Aesop's Fables (1700's), "The Lion and His Fellow Hunters," in which other animals help a lion kill a stag (male deer), but the lion does not share the meat • take the largest portion	Even though Bill was a very talented athlete, it was hard to see him *get the lion's share of the awards.*
126. as red as a **rooster**	ORIGIN: really referring to the color of a rooster's comb on top of its head NOT the rooster; as red as a rooster's (comb) • to be really red	The little boy used food coloring to make his hair *as red as a rooster.*
127.as crazy as a **loon**	ORIGIN: this bird (Common North American Loon) makes a haunting, weird laughing sound; it sounds like the cry of an insane person; the word "loon" is from the word "lunatic", which means an insane person • act/sound crazy or weird https://www.phrases.org.uk/bulletin_board/41/messages/988.html	The old lady who lives across the street is *as crazy as a loon;* she behaves very strangely.
128. as silent/quiet as a **mouse**	• very quiet; unheard	When my cat walks around the house, she's *as quiet as a mouse.*
129. **mouse**y	• plain or dull/timid • not a vibrant color/a dull beige or grey color	My hair is a *mousey* blonde color.
130. play cat and **mouse** with. . .	ORIGIN: refers to the way a cat chases, catches, and then plays with a mouse • torment, tease	When I was trying to win that large business contract, it was *like playing cat and mouse* with the corporation.
131. **monkey** business	ORIGIN: refers to the playful, tricky, mischievous behavior of monkeys • foolish, mischievous, silly behavior	From all the noise in my boys' bedroom, it seems there is a lot of *monkey business* going on.

SIMILIE/EXPRESSION/IDIOM	MEANING	SAMPLE SENTENCE
132. make a **monkey** out of sb.	• make sb. appear stupid/foolish/ridiculous • See #131	The employees at the plant did not like the new manager, so they *made a monkey out of him* by ruining all his projects and plans.
133. **Monkey** see, **monkey** do!	ORIGIN: monkeys often mimic the gestures and behaviors of humans and one another; what it sees, it does • copy someone doing sth.	When the father saw his little boy trying to shave his own face, the father exclaimed, *"Monkey see, monkey do!"*
134. as stubborn as a **mule**	ORIGIN: although quite smart, mules are considered stubborn by their owners because the mules prefer to do things their own way • stubborn, obstinate, rebellious • said about sb. who prefers to do things his own way	Because my wife did not do things the way I expected or wanted her to do, I told her she was *as stubborn as a mule.*
135.as wise as an **owl**	ORIGIN: according to ancient western folklore, the owl is a wise, silent and solitary bird of prey associated with lunar deities - symbols of wisdom, wiser even than the eagle - the totem bird of the Sun Kings. Also, the owl represents the Greek goddess of wisdom, Athena • wise/scholarly/worth listening to https://timesofindia.indiatimes.com/Why-is-the-owl-considered-a-wise-bird-in-the-West-and-a-symbol-of-foolishness-in-India/articleshow/871894.cms	For someone so young, my daughter seems to be *as wise as an owl.*
136. as strong as an **ox**	ORIGIN: an ox is usually a work animal and used to pull heavy loads because of its strength • strong, reliable, capable	Surprisingly, that petite young woman is *as strong as an ox* because she specializes in martial arts.
137. have an **ox** in the ditch	ORIGIN: because an ox is so large, it is very difficult to pull it out of a ditch, especially it it's filled with mud and water • have a very unpleasant/troublesome/difficult situation that's not easily solved	When the lawyer read the will to the greedy adult children, he declared, *"We have an ox in the ditch."* because he realized the son had been left out of his father's will and the lawyer thought it might be a big mistake.

SIMILIE/EXPRESSION/IDIOM	MEANING	SAMPLE SENTENCE
138. The world's [your] **oyster**!	ORIGIN: from a line in Shakespeare's play, <u>The Merry Wives of Windsor</u> but was originally, "the world's [mine] oyster" • you can take/have whatever you want • you have the advantage https://www.quora.com/What-is-the-origin-of-the-phrase-the-world-is-your-oyster	An anonymous person won the recent lottery of over a half billion dollars, and he probably believes that *the world is his oyster*. . .for now.
139. as proud as a **peacock**	ORIGIN: when a male peacock is courting a female, he struts around with his all his feathers fanned out to show how big and marvelous he is, and worthy of her attention • proud, vain • strutting around arrogantly	The new father of triplet girls couldn't resist the temptation to strut around in the hospital; he was definitely as *proud as a peacock*.
140. **piggy**-back	ORIGIN: meaning to carry sth. on one's back, this phrase actually began as "pick (pitch/put) pack"; then through careless use, the words morphed into "pig back" and then "piggy-back"; so this has really nothing to do with pigs • describes sb. on one's shoulders or back http://www.worldwidewords.org/qa/qa-pig3.htm	The children love it when their father carries them *piggy-back*.
141. **pig** out	ORIGIN: pigs can be sloppy, noisy eaters of lots of food • to eat a lot of food in a sloppy manner • See #99	The hot-dog eating contest gave everyone a chance *to pig out*.
142. When **pigs** fly!	ORIGIN: obviously, pigs don't fly, so this refers to an impossible situation • a comment made about sth. that will probably never/unlikely happen • intention to prevent sth. from happening	When the young man asked the girl he liked to go to a movie with him, she said, *"When pigs fly!"*
143. a one-trick **pony**	ORIGIN: ponies often are trained to perform before crowds, sometimes with only one trick • said of sb. who has few friends/talents/skills	Sadly, the girls all thought that young man was rather *like a one-trick pony*; they didn't think he had much to offer.

SIMILIE/EXPRESSION/IDIOM	MEANING	SAMPLE SENTENCE
144. It's a one-**pony** show/circus.	ORIGIN: sometimes signs advertise a "spectacular" show/circus that turns out to be a very small with only one trained animal • not a big deal at all • unimpressive, inconsequential	When all the crowds came to see the magician in town, they were rather disappointed at the *one-pony show*; he had no new tricks.
145. as fast as a **rabbit**	ORIGIN: a rabbit can actually run from 40-73 kph • having the ability to run fast https://www.bunnyslippers.com/blog/bunny-facts-how-fast-can-a-rabbit-run/	That little two-year old was *as fast as a rabbit* and could get into trouble before his mom even knew he was gone.
146. a **rabbit** trail	ORIGIN: refers to the random, wandering, misleading, circular path a rabbit often travels • a pointless, endless argument • a conversation, discussion, or search that seems to lead nowhere	When the husband tried to give his wife a good-sounding excuse for where he had been for three hours, he led her on *a rabbit trail*.
147. pull a **rabbit** out of a hat	ORIGIN: refers to a common magic trick in which a magician pulls a live rabbit out of an apparently empty hat • perform the impossible • find a surprising solution to a problem	The young man unexpectedly received an acceptance to the college he really wanted to attend; it was as if someone had *pulled a rabbit out of a hat*.
148. go down a **rabbit** hole	ORIGIN: from Alice's Adventures in Wonderland by Lewis Carrol; refers to Alice falling down a hole and into an endlessly twisting tunnel underground • an entry into the unknown/difficult/strange • start a mysterious journey	Going into a new culture for the first time can often feel like *going down a rabbit's hole*—so many unknowns, new discoveries, and new expectations..
149. like **rats** deserting a sinking ship	ORIGIN: it is said that rats can sense danger coming and know when to flee for safety; it's not because they're afraid of water • leave an activity or organization that is failing while you still have a choice/chance • hurry and leave in order to avoid getting caught up in difficulties or problems	When students sensed that the college was going to change the entire grading system, they left *like rats deserting a sinking ship*.

SIMILIE/EXPRESSION/IDIOM	MEANING	SAMPLE SENTENCE
150. a **rat** race	ORIGIN: refers to rats running through a maze to try and get the prize of cheese at the end • a pointless, frenzied pursuit with little reward	Working in that factory with all the internal competition and such little pay is *a rat race*.
151. smell a **rat**	ORIGIN: rats often inhabit places where they shouldn't be, and when they die there, they will give off a very unpleasant odor, which would cause sb. to be suspicious and investigate • to be suspicious of sth./sb.	When the promotion didn't go to Maria as promised, her coworker said, *"I smell a rat."*
152. **rat** out/on someone	• report sb. to an authority because of sth. incriminating	My sister knew that Jonathan had stolen my father's car, so she *ratted him out* to the police.
153. strut around like a banty **rooster**	ORIGIN: Banty roosters are small, aggressive chickens that walk around in a rather stiff, arrogant manner • "show off" • usually said of the way a small man is walking in order to feel and look more important	That small man has apparently never felt comfortable with his size because he *struts around like a banty rooster*, and other people laugh at him.
154. packed in like **sardines**	ORIGIN: sardines are tiny fish and commonly packed very tightly in flat tins • to be very crowded in small spaces • often forced crowding	The concert hall is built to comfortably hold about 1000 people; however, for this special concert, the organizers *packed* 3000 of us *in like sardines*.
155. like a **sheep** among wolves	ORIGIN: Matthew 10:16 (New Testament); sheep are innocent and vulnerable; wolves are predators • being in a hostile area/unwelcomed • among a group of people not eager to hear what you have to say or do	When the soft-spoken police official delivered the unwelcomed news to the crowd, he was *like a sheep among wolves*; people were angry that the shooter had not been found guilty of the murder.
156. follow like **sheep**	ORIGIN: sheep do not act independently; they follow the orders and direction of the shepherd; they are easily led and follow each other • to not think for oneself	People often vote in elections without knowing much about the candidates, so they *follow* the recommendations of others *like sheep*.

SIMILIE/EXPRESSION/IDIOM	MEANING	SAMPLE SENTENCE
	• follow the crowd • want to be/think like everyone else	
157. **sheep**ish	ORIGIN: sheep tend to be timid and shy, not very aggressive • timid/shy/non-aggressive • reluctant to start an action or conversation	I was a bit *sheepish* when I asked the store owner for a job because I thought I was too young to work.
158. separate the **sheep** from the goats	ORIGIN: Matthew 25:31 (New Testament); sheep are considered to be gentle, docile, compliant animals whereas goats are considered to be unruly and coarse animals; sheep = good/goats = bad • divide the good from the bad, the reputable from the disreputable • choose those who are qualified for a specific task or position from those who are not	When it was time to select a small group of people to meet with the king, an official commented that it was time *to separate the sheep from the goats.*
159. count **sheep**	ORIGIN: when sharing grazing land, shepherds had to count their own sheep each evening to keep track of their own herd; in doing so, they could very well fall asleep • count imaginary sheep in your mind in order to fall asleep • a tedious, useless process	Because there was no device to keep track of all the people coming into the auditorium, the man had to count each person himself; it was like *counting sheep.*
160. He's the black **sheep** of the family.	ORIGIN: most sheep are white colored due to a dominant gene; If they are born black, it's because of a recessive gene, seen as a negative trait; the sheep stands out from the herd and can be ignored by other sheep; black wool cannot be dyed; often viewed as a sign of the devil • sb. who is considered to be different from the group in a negative or undesirable way • a disreputable person	Sadly, the young man was considered to be the *black sheep of the family* because he wouldn't conform to what was expected of him and often brought shame to his family by his behavior.

SIMILIE/EXPRESSION/IDIOM	MEANING	SAMPLE SENTENCE
161. a **snake** in the grass	ORIGIN: a snake hiding in the grass can be a danger to sb. walking nearby; it remains unseen before striking • sb. who deceives others into trusting him • a person who conceals his motives until ready to act, usually to harm sth. or sb. else.	All these years in the office, that quiet employee was waiting for his chance to take revenge on his manager for never promoting him; he was a real *snake in the grass*.
162. If it were a **snake**, it would've bitten you.	ORIGIN: see #161 • sth. very close to you that goes unseen	My father was always misplacing his newspaper, which was usually very close to his chair; my mom always said, *"If it were a snake, it would've bitten you."*
163. as graceful as a **swan**	ORIGIN: swans seem to glide across the water in a smooth, graceful, effortless manner; however, their feet are paddling very hard under the water • smooth, graceful • sth. seen as effortless without regard to the hard work or preparation beforehand	She worked long, hard hours to master difficult steps to become a successful dancer, but her dancing appeared effortless, and she was *as graceful as a swan*.
164. like having a **tiger** by the tail	ORIGIN: if you grab a tiger by the tail, you are trying to hold onto a powerful and fierce animal, much stronger than yourself; even though you think you're controlling it, it can cause you harm • managing sth. considered to be unmanageable or uncontrollable • unpredictably difficult	For someone who is trying to invest in the stock market for the first time, it may seem *like having a tiger by the tail*; it is so unpredictable.
165. put a **tiger** in [your] tank	ORIGIN: although seen earlier, this was popularized in 1965 by an Exxon Mobile gasoline ad suggesting their brand could provide greater fuel energy and efficiency for your car; tigers are seen as swift, powerful animals • increase [your] energy or efficiency • energize https://blog.oxforddictionaries.com/2015/07/29/tiger-terms-phrases/	Giving him that new job promotion was *like putting a tiger in his tank*.

SIMILIE/EXPRESSION/IDIOM	MEANING	SAMPLE SENTENCE
166. A **tiger** cannot change its stripes.	See #123 • refers to our inability to change our basic nature	*A tiger cannot change its stripes* any better than you can change your family background.
167. as slow as a **turtle**	ORIGIN: turtles are very slow, methodical, deliberate animals • cautious, slow, careful	Sometimes in trying to be a careful and law-abiding driver, my husband drives *as slow as a turtle*.
168. **weasel** out of/into something	ORIGIN: weasels are long, narrow , flexible animals with the skillful ability to get in and out of very small, tight places • easily get out of/into a situation using deceitful/dishonest means • seen as negative/deceptive behavior	After agreeing to be the chairman of the committee, the young woman *weaseled out of it* by lying that she had to take care of her sick mother.
169. You **weasel**!	See #168 • said about sb. who is crafty and clever • said about sb. who is able to get out of unpleasant situations using deceptive means • depending upon one's tone of voice, this could be a negative or slightly complimentary comment	Mike's friend said, *"You Weasel!"* after Mike lied to his boss about being sick and hopped on a bus to go away for the weekend.
170. a **whale** of a . . .	ORIGIN: whales are extraordinarily large mammals • unusually large or long	That was *a whale of a tale* the little boy told about being chased by a bear in the woods.
171. a lone **wolf**	ORIGIN: a wolf is normally a pack animal and travels together with other wolves; unusual for it to travel alone • sb. who stays by himself and doesn't like groups	After being kicked out of the organization for not following the group's rules, Gary started being a *lone wolf*.

SIMILIE/EXPRESSION/IDIOM	MEANING	SAMPLE SENTENCE
172. a **wolf** in sheep's clothing	ORIGIN: proverb originating in the Bible (Matthew 7:15) and describes people acting contrary to their real nature or character and with whom contact could be dangerous; one's basic nature, however, can eventually be seen through the disguise or pretense • pretend to be someone you're not for deceitful reasons • appear to be kind when real intent is to do harm	The gunman was really *a wolf in sheep's clothing* the day he pretended to be the school's janitor and later killed two teachers.
173. throw someone to the **wolves**	ORIGIN: from an Aesop Fable in which a nurse threatens to throw a child to the wolves unless he behaves • abandon sb. to a dangerous situation • protect yourself at the expense of someone else's safety • leave sb. unprotected	The students in the research group no longer wanted to work on the project, so they basically *threw Robert to the wolves* by lying to their professor that Robert had not done any work.
174. cry "**Wolf!**"/cry wolf	ORIGIN: from the Aesop Fable, <u>The Boy Who Cried Wolf</u>, a story about a young shepherd boy who continually and falsely yelled for help to keep a wolf from attacking his sheep. The villagers would come to his rescue, but there was no danger. When he really did need their help, they did not come. • falsely warn of danger or ask for help • lie/exaggerate	My little brother never liked to go to bed, so he'd tell my mother that there were bugs or mice in his room; she would come and look and find nothing; he was always *crying wolf*.
175. a book **worm**	ORIGIN: the larva of a wood-boring beetle or other similar insects that feed on the paper and glue in books • sb. who loves books and is always reading • can be a derogatory term for sb. who is always reading and has no time for others	My granddaughter reads a lot; she's a real *book worm*.

SIMILIE/EXPRESSION/IDIOM	MEANING	SAMPLE SENTENCE
176. **worm** [your] way out of/into something	ORIGIN: a worm has a long, flexible body with no bones so it can easily wiggle in and out of tight spaces • skillfully get what you want by being deceptive	In order to meet Jennifer, Bill *wormed his way into* her political committee by lying about his abilities to organize publicity events.

These idioms, similes, phrasal verbs and other expressions based on animals are used frequently in conversation and in informal writing. Including them in your spoken and written English will increase your fluency and your understanding of the English–speaking culture in which you are now living.

1. Do you have animals "hiding" in your spoken and written native language?

2. If so, how do these expressions compare to similar expressions in your native language?

"BODY" LANGUAGE: Expressions Based on the Body

HEAD AND FACE

1. Get [him] out of [my] hair! .... *REMOVE WHATEVER/WHOEVER IS BOTHERING/ANNOYING SB.*

2. They had a real <u>head to head</u> confrontation. ....*A VERY CLOSE, INTENSE, CONVERSATION/ARGUMENT*

3. The supervisor told him <u>to keep his head above water</u>. .... *TO STAY OUT OF TROUBLE*

4. If we <u>put our heads together</u>, we could figure it out. .... *TO SOLVE A PROBLEM TOGETHER/COLLABORATE*

5. <u>Heads up</u>! ....*A WARNING; PAY ATTENTION; FOR YOUR INFORMATION*

6. His mother <u>gave [him] a real brow-beating</u>. ....*TO ANGRILY CRITICIZE SOMEONE TO THEIR FACE*

7. **I know he's in love because [his] <u>head is in the clouds</u>.** .... ***NOT THINKING CLEARLY/DAY DREAMING***

8. <u>Two heads are better than one</u>. ....*IT'S BETTER TO COLLABORATE/TO SOLVE A PROBLEM TOGETHER/BRAINSTORM*

9. I must talk to him <u>face to face</u>. ....*IN PERSON*

10. The new guy on the assembly line <u>caught [the supervisor's] eye</u>. .... *TO GET THE FAVORABLE ATTENTION OF SOMEONE; TO IMPRESS SOMEONE*

11. He <u>has eyes for</u> [her]. .... *TO THINK SOMEONE IS ATTRACTIVE TO LOOK AT*

12. The son and his father no longer <u>see eye to eye</u> about the government. ....*TO AGREE/HAVE THE SAME OPINION*

13. They were arguing <u>nose to nose</u> over the new job. .... *PHYSICALLY VERY CLOSE TO ONE ANOTHER*

14. Her <u>nose was out of joint</u>. .... *UPSET ABOUT SOMETHING*

15. <u>Keep [your] nose clean</u>!" .... *DO NOTHING TO CAUSE TROUBLE OR SUSPICION*

16. He's <u>down in the mouth.</u> ....*SAD OR DISAPPOINTED AND SHOWING IT ON YOUR FACE*

17. He has a <u>dirty mouth</u>. .... *OFFENSIVE LANGUAGE*

18. It was a <u>tongue-in-check</u> comment. ....*HUMOROUS ALTHOUGH SOUNDING SERIOUS*

19. I was told <u>to hold my tongue</u> at the meeting. ....*TO NOT SAY ANYTHING ABOUT AN ISSUE*

20. You need to <u>have/keep a stiff upper lip.</u> ....*TO SHOW NO EMOTIONS UNDER STRESS*

21. Chin-up! ....*BE BRAVE IN THE FACE OF DIFFICULT SITUATIONS*

22. He took it on the chin. ....*TO TAKE HARSH CRITICISM FROM SOMEONE WITHOUT REACTION*

23. The announcement fell on deaf ears. ....*TO GO UNHEARD; TO BE IGNORED*

24. I saw them dancing cheek to cheek. ....*WITH CHEEKS TOUCHING*

25. The horses were neck and neck. ....*PARALLEL TO ONE ANOTHER; EVEN*

26. The employee is a real pain in the neck. ....*STH./SB. ANNOYING OR BOTHERSOME*

UPPER BODY

27. She was miserable until he got it off [his] chest. ....*REVEAL A STRESSFUL CONCERN/CONFESS*

28. He] holds the key to [her] heart. ....*TO BE TRUSTED BY SOMEONE; TO BE SOMEONE'S CONFIDANT*

29. You have a spot in [my] heart. ....*TO ESPECIALLY LIKE SOMEONE; TO BE A FAVORITE*

30. It's time for us to have a heart to heart talk. ....*AN INTIMATE, PERSONAL CONVERSATION*

31. She has a broken heart. ....*TO FEEL SAD ABOUT STH. OR FOR SB.*

32. We were standing so close, we were shoulder to shoulder. ....*SHOULDERS TOUCHING*

33. I will stand shoulder to shoulder **with** [you]. ....*TO BE EMOTIONALLY SUPPORTIVE OF SB.*

34. Her ex-boyfriend gave her the cold shoulder ....*TO DELIBERATELY IGNORE SOMEONE*

35. He can't stomach [it] ....*UNABLE TO TOLERATE SOMETHING*

36. He doesn't have the stomach for [it]. ....*UNABLE TO TOLERATE SOMETHING*

37. When she jumped into the water, she did a belly flop. ....*TO HIT THE WATER ON YOUR STOMACH*

38. He wanted to tell his father, "Get off my back!" ....*TO STOP CRITICIZING SB.*

39. His back is against the wall; he will have to confess. ....*TO BE PRESSURED TO REVEAL SOMETHING; TO HAVE NO OTHER CHOICE*

40. I have [your]back. ....*TO SUPPORT/PROTECT SB.*

41. Her appointments were all back to back. ....*ONE RIGHT AFTER THE NEXT; CONSECUTIVE*

ARMS, HANDS, FINGERS, LEGS, FEET, TOES

42. They strolled down the street arm in arm. ....ARMS LINKED

43. She likes to rub elbows with [rich] people. .... TO ENJOY SOCIALIZING WITH A CERTAIN KIND OF PEOPLE

44. She had to wear a brace for her tennis elbow. ....PAINFUL CONDITION OF THE ELBOW DUE TO OVERUSE

45. I saw them walking hand in hand. ....HOLDING ONE ANOTHER'S HAND

46. Hands up! ....AN ORDER GIVEN BY POLICE TO PUT YOUR HANDS OVER YOUR HEAD

47. It's a hands-on project. ....ACTUALLY USING YOUR HANDS TO DO STH./REQUIRING PERSONAL INVOLVEMENT

48. Don't go out with him because he's all hands! .... INAPPROPRIATE TOUCHING OF WOMEN

49. Can you lend [me] a hand? .... TO HELP SOMEONE/ PROVIDE ASSISTANCE

50. Every leader needs a reliable right-hand man. ....SB. WHO IS EFFICIENT/LOYAL/DEPENDABLE/PRODUCTIVE

51. It was dangerous hand to hand combat. ....CLOSE-UP FIGHTING WITH HANDS

52. Many poor children live a hand-to-mouth existence. ....NOT ENOUGH MONEY OR FOOD TO LIVE ON

53. Lisa has always talked with her hands. ....TO GESTURE A LOT WHILE TALKING

54. All hands on board! ....A CALL FOR EVERYONE TO HELP

55. I'll keep my fingers crossed. ....TO PHYSICALLY CROSS ONE'S FINGERS AS A SIGN OF GOOD LUCK/EXPECT STH. GOOD

56. She's all thumbs. ....CLUMSY/LACK OF GOOD EYE-HAND COORDINATION

57. [He] has been on [his] knees about this issue...TO PRAY

58. He just put [his] foot in [his] mouth.. TO SAY SOMETHING EMBARRASSING OR AWKWARD

59. It's time for her children to stand on [their] own two feet.................................TO BE INDEPENDENT/MAKE [THEIR] OWN DECISIONS

60. He had to get some medicine for his athlete's foot. ....A FUNGUS INFECTION ON THE FEET

61. He has always danced with two left feet. ....NOT VERY WELL/CLUMSY

62. His parents thought $1,000.00 would help him get off on the right foot. .... TO START STH. WELL

63. That girl can really <u>think on [her] feet</u>. ...... *TO SPEAK KNOWLEDGEABLY ON A VARIETY OF TOPICS WITH NO PREPARATION*

64. We need to <u>hot foot it out of here</u>!..*TO LEAVE SOME PLACE VERY QUICKLY*

65. I did well in the interview, so I still <u>have [my] foot in the door</u>. ....*TO HAVE AN ADVANTAGE*

66. They <u>were standing toe to toe</u>. ....*TO STAND FACING ONE ANOTHER VERY CLOSELY*

67. He finally <u>put [his] toe across the line</u> ....*TO DO STH. DIFFERENT; TO DARE TO CHANGE STH.*

68. I saw the little girl <u>standing on tippy toes/tiptoes</u>. .... ***TO STAND ON RAISED FEET***

HEARD AT WORK: Work-Related Expressions & Jargon

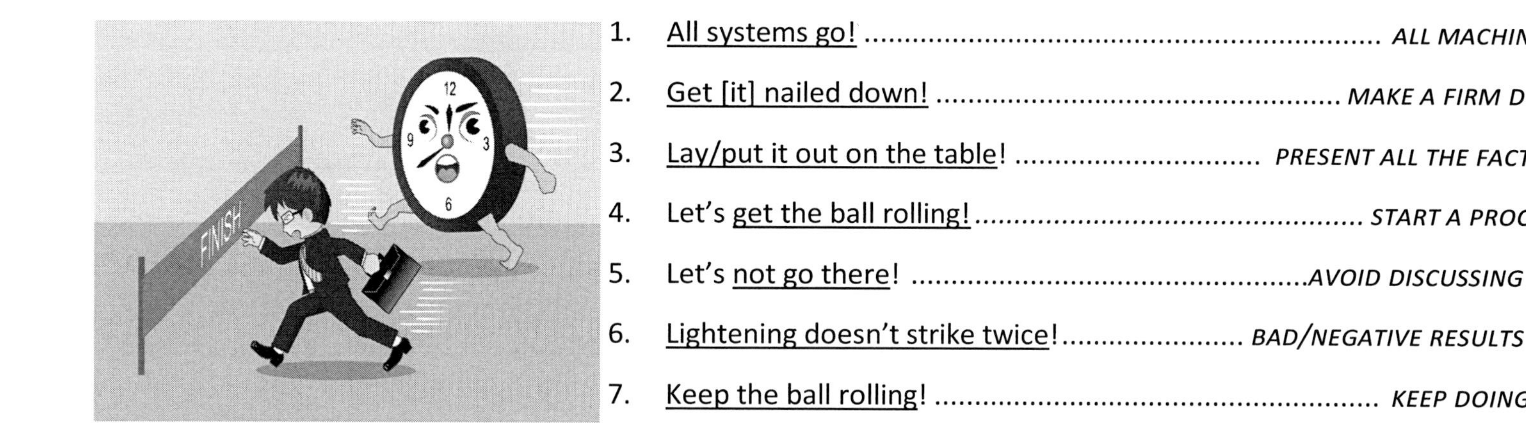

1. <u>All systems go!</u> .... *ALL MACHINERY/ALL CONTROLS ARE OPERATING*

2. <u>Get [it] nailed down!</u> .... *MAKE A FIRM DECISION ABOUT STH./PLAN/PROJECT*

3. <u>Lay/put it out on the table!</u> .... *PRESENT ALL THE FACTS OF A PROJECT/ISSUE AT ONE TIME*

4. Let's <u>get the ball rolling!</u> .... *START A PROCESS/PROCEDURE/SYSTEM/MEETING*

5. Let's <u>not go there!</u> ....*AVOID DISCUSSING A DELICATE OR COMPLICATED ISSUE*

6. <u>Lightening doesn't strike twice!</u> .... *BAD/NEGATIVE RESULTS DO NOT HAPPEN MORE THAN ONCE*

7. <u>Keep the ball rolling!</u> .... *KEEP DOING WHAT YOU'RE DOING; DON'T STOP*

8. It's a <u>race against the clock</u>! ....***AN EFFORT TO FINISH SOMETHING ON TIME/BY A SPECIFIC DEADLINE***

9. Don't <u>spread yourself too thin</u>. ....*DON'T BE SO BUSY THAT YOU NEGLECT IMPORTANT THINGS*

10. <u>Step up to the table!</u> ....*BE CONFIDENT ENOUGH TO PRESENT YOUR IDEAS/RECOMMENDATION/OR OPINION*

VERBS

11. The boss wants us to <u>act like family</u>.. .... *TO INTERACT LIKE A TEAM/A GROUP/A CLOSE-KNIT UNIT*

12. I was <u>banking on</u> getting that raise. .... *TO CONFIDENTLY EXPECT STH. TO HAPPEN*

13. She's <u>beating around the bush</u>. ....*TO TALK INDIRECTLY/NOT IDENTIFY AN ISSUE OR IDEA CLEARLY*

14. It could <u>blow the doors off</u>. ....*TO BE A REALLY BIG SUCCESS*

15. We would be <u>building straw houses and blowing them away</u>.....................................*TO DO SOMETHING TOO QUICKLY ONLY TO HAVE IT FALL APART*

16. I'm tired. I think I'll <u>call it a day</u>. .... *TO QUIT WORK EARLY/TO BE DONE FOR THE DAY*

17. We'll just <u>crank it out</u>. ....*TO WORK HARD TO CREATE/PRODUCE STH.*

18. It never <u>crossed my mind to</u>. .... *TO THINK ABOUT SOMETHING*

19. <u>Cut the results</u> any way you want. ....*TO ANALYZE/EVALUATE/DIVIDE*

20. We can't <u>cut corners</u> in how we clean this building or any building. ....*TO DO STH. IN A CHEAPER/EASIER WAY*

21. [Her work team <u>fell behind </u>its monthly quota. ....*TO FAIL TO MEET A GOAL OR QUOTA*

22. No one can <u>fill [his] shoes</u>..*TO DO THE JOB AS WELL AS THE PREVIOUS PERSON*

23. They could <u>frown on </u>it. ....*DISAPPROVE*

24. We have to <u>get off the dime</u>...*TO START MOVING/BE PRODUCTIVE/SHOW RESULTS*

25. She <u>got the axe</u>. ....*TO BE FIRED*

26. *I think I've <u>got the feel of it</u>. .... TO UNDERSTAND THE PROCESS/PROCEDURE*

27. [He] <u>got [his] wings clipped.</u> .... *TO BE PROHIBITED FROM DOING STH.*

28. We've got to <u>get the wheel spinning on this</u>. .... *TO START MOVING Forward*

29. We need to <u>get [the whole thing] anchored</u> down.................... *TO GET STH. SETTLED/DECIDED/FIXED/FINALIZED*

30. We just <u>got wind of it.</u> .... *TO JUST FIND OUT ABOUT STH/JUST GET THE NEWS*

31. Please <u>go the extra mile</u> and work overtime. .... *TO DO/WORK MORE THAN WHAT IS USUALLY REQUIRED*

32. I think he <u>has a screw loose.</u> .... *TO BE REALLY CONFUSED/INATTENTIVE/"CRAZY"*

33. My supervisor <u>hit the ceiling </u>when she saw the error... *TO BECOME VERY ANGRY*

34. He <u>jumped through all the hoops</u> to get his promotion. . ...*TO DO ALL THE REQUIRED TASKS; TO MEET EXPECTATIONS*

35. We've got to <u>keep turning the wheel on this.</u>.. *TO CONTINUE TO IMPROVE/CHANGE/MODIFY*

36. We'll end up <u>managing the whole puppy.</u> ....*TO BE IN CHARGE OF THE WHOLE PROJECT/DESIGN/ISSUE/DEVELOPMENT*

37. She <u>missed the boat</u> because she didn't respond to the e-mail. .... *TO MISS THE OPPORTUNITY; TO NOT GET ANOTHER CHANCE*

38. We have to <u>move the needle.</u> .... *TO CHANGE/IMPROVE/PROGRESS*

39. We have to <u>nail down</u> the plans for the ceremony. .... *TO MAKE A DECISION/SETTLE ON/DETERMINE THE EXACT DETAILS*

40. It barely <u>pays the lights</u>. .... *TO BRING IN ENOUGH MONEY TO PAY EVEN THE UTILITY BILLS/GENERATE REVENUE*

41. Just don't <u>plant a tree and then chop it down</u>. ....*TO SPEND A LOT OF TIME WORKING ON A PROJECT AND LATER "KILL" OR REJECT IT*

42. The team members <u>put two and two together</u>...*TO FIGURE OUT STH. THAT HAD PREVIOUSLY BEEN CONCEALED*

43. We're <u>riding shotgun</u>. .... *TO PROTECT SYSTEM/PROJECT/PRODUCT FROM PROBLEMS OR CORPORATE HIJACKING*

44. <u>Separate [them] from the herd</u>. ....*TO IDENTIFY AND REMOVE/SEPARATE SB. FROM OTHER EMPLOYEES BASED ON QUALIFICATIONS OR BEHAVIOR*

45. This could really <u>set people off</u>. .... *TO GET SB. IRRITATED/ANNOYED/ANGRY*

46. The new employee <u>spilled the beans</u>. .... *TO UNINTENTIONALLY REVEAL A SECRET OR STH. NOT YET ANNOUNCED*

47. Our supervisor will <u>touch base with</u> [you] next week about the job. .... *TO CONTACT*

48. He's <u>walking a fine line</u>. ....*TO BE ON "PROBATION"/AVOID TROUBLE OR BEING FIRED*

49. Let's <u>walk through this</u>. ....*TO REVIEW PARTICULAR STEPS/PROCESS/PROCEDURE*

PREPOSITIONAL PHRASES

50. These are difficult negotiations so we're doing everything <u>by the book</u>. ....*ACCORDING TO RULES/INSTRUCTIONS*

51. [My job] is <u>in the bag</u>. .... *FOR CERTAIN*

52. This report belongs <u>in the circular file</u>. ....*IN THE WASTE BASKET*

53. <u>On a scale of 1 to 10</u>, he's a 7. ....*A LINEAR WAY OF RATING EXCELLENCE OR SUCCESS; 10 BEING THE BEST*

54. My boss is always <u>on edge</u>. .... *IRRITABLE/ANNOYED*

55. **He's still <u>on the fence</u> about accepting the new contract.** .... ***UNDECIDED/NOT SURE WHICH SIDE OF AN ISSUE TO BE ON***

56. I need everyone <u>on the same page</u> before we change schedules. .... *IN AGREEMENT ABOUT STH./CONSENSUS*

57. It's still <u>up in the air</u>. .... *UNDECIDED; UNPREDICTABLE*

NOUNS

58. All those difficulties last year became <u>agents for good</u>. ....*PEOPLE /DEVELOPMENTS BENEFICIAL TO A PROJECT/PROCESS/COMPANY*

59. That new gardener is <u>a ball of fire</u>; the park is beautiful! ....*AN ENERGETIC/PRO-ACTIVE PERSON*

60. That electrical system was <u>a benchmark</u> 20 years ago. .... *THE ORIGINAL STANDARD/REFERENCE POINT THAT IS USED TO EVALUATE SUCCESS*

61. <u>The bottom line</u> is we can't afford to give our technicians a raise. ....*THE FINAL EXPLANATION/THE "LAST WORD"*

62. We need to get buy-in from the staff first. .... *COMMENTS FROM OTHERS INVOLVED IN A PROJECT SO THEY WILL HAVE "OWNERSHIP"*

63. For a change of pace, let's start cleaning the rooms at 8:00 AM. .... *CHANGE THE USUAL SPEED OR SEQUENCE OF STH.*

64. The new HR Director wants to do a cultural audit. .... *EVALUATION OF WORKPLACE CULTURE: MORALE/INTERPERSONAL COMMUNICATIONS*

65. The new Marketing Director wants to take [our] corporate pulse. .... *EVALUATION OF THE HEALTH/ROI OF A COMPANY OR CORPORATION*

66. Thankfully, we have those hard contracts in place. .... *CONTRACTS THAT are FIXED/UNWAVERING/INFLEXIBLE/FINALIZED*

67. Talking about the supervisor's drinking problem is a loaded gun. .... *A VERY DELICATE/SENSITIVE/CONTROVERSIAL ISSUE*

68. Our salesmen need to take advantage of all that low-hanging fruit. .... *CLIENTS/CONTACTS/PRODUCTS/REVENUE EASILY OBTAINED*

69. The key to making [this] happen is cutting overtime pay. ....*A PARTICULAR EFFORT THAT ACCOMPLISHES A DESIRED GOAL*

70. The piece I don't understand is why we don't hire another manager. ....*A PARTICULAR PART OF A PLAN /DOCUMENT/PROJECT*

71. The ramp-up to our new facility is going well. .... *PREPARATION OF A NEW PROJECT/COMPANY/SYSTEM/PROCEDURE*

72. Offering ESL classes to your employees will positively impact your ROI. .... *THE RETURN ON INVESTMENT*

73. The roll-out of our new campaign will be next Tuesday. ......*THE LAUNCH OF A NEW PRODUCT/PROJECT/SYSTEM/PROCEDURE*

74. The roll-up of all those bankrupt companies is about to begin. ....*A MERGER/ACQUISITION OF SMALLER COMPANIES*

75. Our CEO didn't like [their] sell to us about that new software. .... *A PRESENTATION/SALES PITCH/NEGOTIATION*

76. [My] sense is that we will increase revenue in the third quarter. ....*A FEELING/UNDERSTANDING/OPINION*

77. We need CNAs who have good soft skills. .... *SKILLS THAT AREN'T EASILY TAUGHT: INTERPERSONAL/TEAM MANAGEMENT*

78. **It's a complete snore to me**. ....*STH. VERY BORING/UNINTERESTING*

79. Getting these new systems in place will please all our stakeholders. ....*THE PEOPLE MOST INTERESTED/INVESTED IN STH.*

80. [My] take about the floor nurse is that she's really stressed about lack of staff. .... *A PERCEPTION/UNDERSTANDING*

81. The night and day managers always argue over turf issues. .... *ISSUES CONCERNING ONLY A PARTICULAR AREA OR GROUP*

82. We need a two-pronged approach from Admin and Housekeeping. .... *AN ATTEMPT TO SOLVE A PROBLEM FROM TWO DIFFERENT DIRECTIONS*

83. The staff meeting produced a real witches' brew of impossible goals. .... *AN ODD/ INCOMPATIBLE MIXTURE OF IDEAS/ITEMS/PEOPLE*

84. [He's] <u>asleep at the wheel</u>. .... *NOT PAYING ATTENTION TO MONITORS/RESPONSIBILITIES*

85. We're <u>ahead of the game/curve</u> in getting our TV ads out. ....*IN FRONT OF THE COMPETITION*

86. **I don't think I'm <u>cut out to [be a groundskeeper]</u>.**..*BE PREPARED /QUALIFIED/SKILLED TO DO STH.*

87. We'll be <u>left to run the show</u>. ....*BE IN CHARGE OF THE WHOLE PROJECT*

88. Let's get [these new computers] <u>up and running</u>. ....*OPERATIONAL/FUNCTIONAL*

TEXT CREDITS & COMMENTS

Page 3   My students always have a fairly good grasp of frequency adverbs but tend not to experiment with other adverbs. This list was adapted from http://www.core-corner.com/Web2/FreeDownload/k2qd717v_20090720.pdf.

Page 5   Article usage remains a mystery for students even at the higher levels. This chart was adapted from THEWLIS. *Grammar Dimensions 3, Platinum Edition*, 3E. © 2000 Heinle/ELT, a part of Cengage Learning, Inc. www.cengage.com/permissions Used with permission. My students found the original chart too complicated, so we collectively modified it.

Page 11   This chart is based on content in VAN ZANTE, JANIS , Grammar Links 3, A Theme-Based Course for Reference and Practice, pp. 390-394, ©2005 Houghton Mifflin Co., Cengage Learning. Used with permission. Verbs/adjectives are divided into "brain" verbs/adjectives, "emotional" verbs/adjectives, "sensory" verbs/adjectives, and all those verbs that introduce speech.

Page 11   Because my students had difficulty remembering all the information on Noun Clauses in the textbook, I created this one-page summary, adapting the content from VAN ZANTE, JANIS , Grammar Links 3, A Theme-Based Course for Reference and Practice, pp. 390-394, 397; ©2005 Houghton Mifflin Co., Cengage Learning. Used with permission.

Page 61-63 These charts consolidate and reformat content in VAN ZANTE, JANIS, Grammar Links 3, A Theme-Based Course for Reference and Practice, pp. 349-361 and 82-115 respectively, ©2005 Houghton Mifflin Co., Cengage Learning. Used with permission.

Page 67   This chart consolidates and reformats "perfect modals" content in VAN ZANTE, JANIS, Grammar Links 3, A Theme-Based Course for Reference and Practice, pp. 293-300, ©2005 Houghton Mifflin Co., Cengage Learning. Used with permission. I have changed the terms "Social Modals" and "Belief Modals" because my students never related to those terms.

Page 83-84   Changing quoted speech to reported speech is often a complicated exercise for students, and although textbooks that I have used present all the information, I found that presenting the information in this chart was easier for my students to grasp and use as a reference. This chart was adapted from content in VAN ZANTE, JANIS, Grammar Links 3, A Theme-Based Course for Reference and Practice, pp. 405-413, ©2005 Houghton Mifflin Co., Cengage Learning. Used with permission.

Page 86   Although you can find many iterations of this on the internet, I adapted and modified the version found in ORION, GERTRUDE, Pronouncing American English: Sounds, Stress, and Intonation, 3rd Edition, p.115, ©2012 Heinle, Cengage Learning. Used with permission.

Page 92   I started using theses two examples of punctuation many years ago to clarify for my students how important punctuation is. They frequently recite the letters in front of the class. Doing so made them easier to understand. It also was an interesting opportunity to introduce the history of the "Dear John" letter. According to Games Publications, "The Dear John letter appeared as part of a contest in the January 1984 issue of Games." ©Games Publications, Fort Washington, PA 19034; Gloria Rosenthal, Games, January, 1984; games@kappapublishing.com   Used with permission.

Page 100   This poem has been circulating for over twenty years, and I began using it in 1994 to teach my students to pay attention to homophones and to not solely rely on their Spell Checker as this function became more available on computers. I have only used these particular verses and recently discovered on www.grammar.about.com that Richard Nordquist attributes them to Mark Eckman, who apparently wrote them in a newsletter called, "AT&T Today" in 1991, when he was an AT&T employee. Shortly after that, Jerrold H. Zar expanded these two verses into a much longer poem entitled "Candidate for a Pullet Surprise." According to Jerrold H. Zar, the two verses used here "are NOT those that [Mark Eckman] wrote, though they are similar." These have "several words different from those used by Eckman or me, and the rhythm and pronunciation of the poem is not as good as in Eckman's version." They nevertheless serve a useful purpose.

Page 131-137 This classic tongue twister has apparently been around since 1909 alternatively as "The Rhapsody of Esau Wood", (Evening Post, Vol LXXVIII, Issue 39, August 14, 1909, p. 10) and "The Story of Esau Wood" and attributed to W.E. Southwick in WELLS, CAROLYN, Such Nonsense! An Anthology, George Doran Company, New York, 1918, p.180. I adapted and modified the version in ORION, GERTRUDE, Pronouncing American English: Sounds, Stress, and Intonation, 3rd Edition, p.66, ©2012 Heinle, Cengage Learning. Used with permission. I had discovered that my students had no context for saws and sawing wood, so trying to make sense of this story was too difficult for them since appropriate intonation, stress, and rhythm occur in context. Therefore, making this easier for them to manage and adding pictures suddenly gave the exercise new life and purpose.

IMAGE CREDITS

Page 2   ©FAMILY CIRCUS ©1994 Bil Keane, Inc. Dist. By King Features Synd.

Page 11   ©Can Stock Photo Inc. #9965353.jpg/brain ©focalpoint

123rf.com # 3550093 <a href='http://www.123rf.com/profile_dragon_fang'>dragon_fang / 123RF Stock Photo</a>/ faces

123rf.com #21822836 <a href='http://www.123rf.com/profile_Krisdog'>Krisdog / 123RF Stock Photo</a>/eye

123rf.com #9818943 <a href='http://www.123rf.com/profile_ninell'>ninell / 123RF Stock Photo</a> /ear

©Can Stock Photo Inc. #2469926.jpg/people ©michaeldb; www.canstockphoto.com

Page 25   Shutterstock_647573074.jpg.; Shutterstock_260827349.jpg; www.shutterstock.com

Page 26   Shutterstock_31530592.jpg ©Freud; www.shutterstock.com

Page 27   Clipartof.com #10671_smjpg_519148502v802104V.jpg ©COLLC0015

Page 31   Moziru.com/farm animals-clipart-2

Page 43   clipartof.com #54645_BLOGJPG.jpg, #54610_BLOGJPG.jpg, ©COLLC0108

Page 63   123rf.com #2852667 <a href='http://www.123rf.com/profile_higyou'>higyou / 123RF Stock Photo</a>

Page 64   ©FAMILY CIRCUS ©2000 Bil Keane, Inc. Dist. By King Features Synd.

Page 67   123rf.com #26769146/top   <a href='http://www.123rf.com/profile_mrgrafi'>mrgrafi / 123RF Stock Photo</a>

123rf.com #26769177/bottom   <a href='http://www.123rf.com/profile_mrgrafi'>mrgrafi / 123RF Stock Photo</a>

Page 82   ©Robert Leighton, www.robert-leighton.com Used with permission.

Page 86   Colourbox #3507071; www.colourbox.com

Page 87   Shutterstock_100550416.jpg, ©3drenderings; www.shutterstock.com

Page 89   Shutterstock_340732577.jpg/Shutterstock_273904649.jpg Shutterstock_259908173.jpg

Shutterstock_295946375.jpg; www.shutterstock.com

Page 91   Shutterstock_668724652.jpg; www.shutterstock.com

Page 94   ©Can Stock Photo Inc./clairev; © Can Stock Photo Inc./lenm; www.canstockphoto.com

Page 97   Images hand drawn by Melanie Douglas, ©2014. Used with permission.

Page 100   Colourbox #8610123 ©emrCartoons; www.colourbox.com

Page 116   ©SH Chambers www.shchambers.com Used with permission.

Page 117   123rf.com #7510689_ml.jpg/top, bottom ©andres rodriguez; www.123rf.com

123rf.com #14800257_ml.jpg/middle <a href='http://www.123rf.com/profile_higyou'>higyou / 123RF Stock Photo</a

©Corina Rosu

Page 119   123rf.com#26769177©Yael Weiss; www.123rf.com

Page 120   ©Can Stock Photo Inc. # csp15574078; ©linesartpilot; www.canstockphoto.com

Page 126   ©Mark Anderson www.andertoons.com

Page 128   Shutterstock_182181728.jpg ©Rudie Strummer; www.shutterstock.com

Page 130   Colourbox #3553129 ©Yayayoyo; www.colourbox.com

Page 131   Colourbox #7196598 ©Aloysius Patrimonio; www.colourbox.com

Page 132   Depositphotos_9023648_s.jpg/pile of three logs; Depositphotos_9405598_s.jpg/lumberjack

Page 133   Depositphotos_9405598_s.jpg/lumberjack; Depositphotos_39399043_s.jpg/log; Depositphotos_28836089_s.jpg/ chainsaw; www.depositphotos.com

Page 134   Depositphotos_12794619_s.jpg/chainsaw; Depositphotos_9023648_s.jpg/pile of three logs; www.depositphotos.com

Page 135   Depositphotos_9023648_s.jpg/pile of three logs; Depositphotos_9405598_s.jpg/lumberjack; www.depositphotos.com

Page 136   Depositphotos_9405598_s.jpg/lumberjack; Depositphotos_39399043_s.jpg/log; Depositphotos_28836089_s.jpg/ chainsaw; www.depositphotos.com

Page 137   Depositphotos_12794619_s.jpg/chainsaw; Depositphotos_9023648_s.jpg/pile of three logs; www.depositphotos.com

Page 140   Shutterstock_78298663.jpg; www.shutterstock.com; Shutterstock_1006580396 jpg.©Ksenya Savva/
           www.shutterstock.com; Dreamstime_m_92892381 © Idey; www.dreamstime.com
Page 171   Shutterstock_179621324 jpg. ©Igor Zakowski; www.shutterstock.com
Page 172   https://jenesl760.wordpress.com/2014/05/23/cartoon-friday-body-idioms/get-off-my-back/; David Wilson James
           may be original artist; diligent efforts have yielded no results in securing formal permission although this image
           is available unattributed on the internet
Page 173   https://www.clipartof.com/1044753_jpg.©toonaday
Page 174   Shutterstock_165069950 ©Selena; www.shutterstock.com
Page 175   Dreamstime_m_47867225 jpg.© Soponpotsit; www.dreamstime.com
Page 176   Shutterstock_581953417 .jpg ©Zenzen; www.shutterstock.com
Page 177   Dreamstime_m_23877800 © Brett Lamb; www.dreamstime.com
Page 178   Dreamstime_m_88915264.jpg ©Tereeez; www.dreamstime.com
Page 179   Shutterstock_112039931.jpg ©Lightspring; www.shutterstock.com;